THE MUMBAI MASSACRE

60 HOURS OF TERROR

The muzlumz first stop on their "2008 - 2009 Christian Holiday World Terror Tour"

Written
By

DAVID J. FORGIONE
M.S.,M.A.,M.B.A.,C.T.S.,P.I.

Published December 5th, 2008

3

Copyright Page

978-0-557-03250-1
ISBN Number

LIBRARY OF CONGRESS Control Number = **2009903715**

This book is dedicated to peace for all mankind

May all nations find peace within

May we all start behaving as this life should be lived....

As a

"Pure Act"

A Note from the Author

This is a "blog book". This is a very unscientific and un-academic historical story written by me. There was no academic peer review done on this book. Academia will probably not like this book. There are no sources to quote from other than I got all my information from 60 hours of watching TV and using the internet to gather unverifiable information. This is where I was able to gain the information necessary to tell this story. This "blog book", is to be distinguished from an academic publication. I am not trying to prove or establish any theory other than this event in Mumbai took place during the month of November 2008. Perhaps the information in this book is true and perhaps some of it is not. The only proof I have that this event really took place are the pictures taken of this event and the minimal story the U.S. news media told us in the U.S. But, this is the only work out there at this moment regarding this event and this story needs to be told.

This is my personal interpretation of what the world media related to the world, during this event.

Perhaps someone in Mumbai will read this story and contact me. Perhaps I can co-author with this person who can supply pictures of this event and their story. At that time I will release a second edition of this book. I think this story is too important to wait to tell. There were too many mistakes made by the Indian government in their handling of this event for the story to wait to be told. I see this event as a link in a chain of global terrorist events which is part of a global war being waged at this very moment.

So, here it is, my historical "blog book" account of the events that took place in Mumbai, India, during the U.S holiday of Thanksgiving in November 2008 – the first stop on the muzlum "2008-2009 Christian Holiday World Terror Tour".

KEY TO ABBREVIATIONS

K = a thousand…..4K is four thousand

M = a million……..$4M is four million dollars

B = a billion………$4B is four billion dollars

T = a trillion………$4T is four trillion dollars

MM = the Mumbai Massacre

muzlum - a follower of Islam and "the sharia" code of Islamic Law - who believes in the religious necessity of the mass murder of innocents to accomplish a one government Islamic/sharia - governed world

To be distinguished from a –

Muslim – one who believes in the Islamic religion but does not believe in the mass murder of innocents

The Muslim does not believe in the literal interpretation of "the sharia" code of law. A literal interpretation which declares that the mass murder of all innocents who are not "followers of the sharia and Islam" is religiously justified, (be them innocents or not - or Muslim or not).

Innocents – those that have not taken up arms – those not involved in fighting. For example, people riding a commuter train to work during rush hour - would be an example of a group of "innocents" on a train going to work.

TABLE OF CONTENTS

ABOUT THE AUTHOR

David Forgione is a retired autoworker from Detroit, Michigan, U.S.A. - currently seeking a full or part time teaching or consulting position.

Books written by David are available in worldwide distribution with an ISBN identifier and at http://stores.lulu.com/djforgione and www.amazon.com

- **The Mumbai Massacre**
- **Anarchy in Athens**
- **Getting Even in Gaza**
- **When Cars Burned Gas – The First 31 Days**
- **When Cars Burned Gas – The Series – Volume I – The First 77 Days – Transition to Power**
- **When Cars Burned Gas –Volume II – The First 100 Days –The President Takes Oath: Revolution of Hope**

David is licensed by the State of Michigan as a Private Investigator and has degrees from:

Birmingham Brother Rice H.S.

Western Michigan University -   B.A. – Philosophy and Religion Majors

University of Detroit Mercy -   M.S., M.A., M.B.A.

Specs Howard School
    of Broadcast Arts -   Broadcast Arts Technical Certification

InfoComm University -   C.T.S. – Certified Technical Specialist

djforgione@hotmail.com

FORWARD

I was involved in another project and just happened to be watching the start of this event on TV. I became obsessed with the need to know "the how and the why this event with - multiple simultaneous targets - could have happened". I answered this question in my mind and you'll find some answers here in this book.

Someone studying this event needs to absorb all the facts and theories – from all sources - and come up with their own conclusions regarding the precipitate events and what actually occurred here and why.

This is a story about the most complex and multi-faceted terrorist attack in modern times – in some ways worse than the "passenger airplanes into tall buildings scenario".

Perhaps this was step one in a larger global plan of sending a group of terrorists from country to country on a "world tour of terror". 6.5 days after the end of this event Greece is torn by riots for 21 straight days, (from December 5th to December 26th). On December 27th Israel attacks the Gaza Strip and the Greek riots end as the "world terror tour" gets back to its roots – back to Gaza - to get even. (The title of my latest book)

This Mumbai event takes place over the Thanksgiving holiday weekend of 2008. Perhaps a motive in the timing of the event was to get USA Thanksgiving Day dinner media news coverage. But what was the message to us here in the USA?

There is no statement of responsibility telling the world who and why this event was staged. Not even the captured terrorist Kasab - gives us a why and if he has revealed this during interrogation- the government of India won't release the why.

We are stuck with studying the targets – the past aggrieved parties - to look for a close fit - and we can always turn to **Dawood Ibrahim** and his international organized crime syndicate the **"D-Gang"** as a prime suspect. That said; During the event we have 2 different terrorist teams at 2 separate siege locations - making 2 separate phone calls to 2 different Indian entities – speaking in 2 different Indian dialects - at 2 different times - asking for 2 very different things. One terrorist asks for the release of all Mujahideens held in India while the other terrorist says he wants the government to talk to him about Kashmir and the killing of Muslims and he'll release the hostages he is holding at his location.

The large majority of these mass murderers – between 10 and 90 - will escape and go to Greece where 6.5 days later they hit multiple targets around Greece and cause the government to shutdown. These riots will go on for over 21 days until Israel attacks the Gaza Strip.

The terrorists would have been shooting in Greece but they left their empty guns back in Mumbai. Instead in Greece they are throwing thousands of Molotov cocktails made from basics: beer bottles filled with 10 ounces of gas with a rag.

One of my books Anarchy in Athens covers this event basically the same way I have covered the Mumbai event.

A very important fact in this book is revealed towards the end – but to cut to the chase – and so you won't miss it:

In Mumbai, India, the local Muslim cemetery refuses to bury the 9 terrorists killed during the Mumbai Massacre.

Islamic custom requires the local Islamic cemetery to accept unclaimed Islamic bodies and to provide a religious burial function after 3 days.

The local Islamic cemetery has stated that these dead terrorists cannot be followers of Islam after committing the inhuman atrocities and the mass murdering of Muslim innocents – and therefore they cannot be buried in an Islamic cemetery.

On top of everyone else who was murdered during this event - this attack also was a muzlum on innocent Muslim killing event.

There is a small hook" to this story I have written. But, to make a point I must tell you a story.

Inside any news service department – where they come up with the news broadcast – "someone" is reading the printout from a computer or teletype machine connected to the "news wire" (i.e. Reuters – Associated Press) services that collect the news and deliver it to their subscribers (i.e. – FOX). Each day there are thousands of news stories to choose from in the global 24 hour a day world.

You might ask – who determines – from all of this "news printout" – what news I am going to receive from my favorite news source – cable, radio stations or print media.

"Someone" in a news center – is reading from an enormous pile of news worthy stories. "Someone" will then "cherry pick" the news – picking stories they think you should hear – and what they think you will want to hear. There are too many stories for you to get them all, (by a thousand).

"Someone" – can if he or she wants - modify the news story they have determined you should hear - to place a "spin" on it. This is to make this news story palatable to the news service provider – her or his employer - and the economic entities that support the specific media news service provider. "Someone" is now creating "newz" with their employer bias attached. This is most easily done by reporting an incomplete news story – a simple omission to obfuscate.

If you have every watched a FOX news story and then compared it to the same CNN news story – you should be able to see a difference in the content and message of the same news stories. CNN has a different "spin" on the news than FOX. Ted Turner (owner of CNN and Headline News) said in a recent interview that CNN and Headline News Networks are left wing and that FOX is a right wing news agency.

Okay so where am I going with this short story? To create the content of this book – I watched TV and accessed the internet. Sources I don't trust. These sources had problems delivering in the middle of this event – from hour 48 to the conclusion. I also turned to foreign – unconfirmed – internet information to complete this story. I have – "no confidence" - in my TV news or internet sources – and just use them to back up or confirm news from one another.

I do not believe 10 to 20% of the information included in this book is the absolute truth. No one should believe any media news source without other news sources to confirm. But, this is the way the world news media wanted me/you/everyone to see this event. So, as reported to the public in the USA and all over the world.......

I have created a story – a historic timeline - of the Mumbai Massacre event – based on simply watching TV and surfing the web. I treated this information source as if they were my "wire service" and as if I were the subscriber. I played the part of the news director deciding what you should read and hear.

I gave it all to you - be it true or false (I probably gave you both). I included "strange" and "conflicting" information as it was delivered to me via the "media" – because I know this is important to the student of terrorism. I tried not to put any "spin" on this "already spun" information.

I am hoping students of terrorism will study this multi-faceted event to insure that mistakes made during this event will not be tolerated and then become repeated in the future. For example before the shooting started – while in route - the event could have been stopped in its tracks by the Indian Coast Guard. Worse, it was known months prior by the Mumbai police – told to them by the head of the Fisherman's Union - that a dark entity might be using some boats belonging to the 1000 small fishing vessel fleet, to smuggle in arms and explosives on a daily basis into Mumbai. (Tens of thousands of rounds of ammunition were needed for multiple persons to fire automatic weapons for 60 hours – I would think a minimum of 100K to 250K rounds were needed)

I am sure there are many other ways to look at this event – on many levels - as one studies attack on innocents as a way to depose and take over a government. Please pay special attention to what information needs to be released to the public and what information should not be released until the end of the event and perhaps never released.

Just a thought - The Granger Causality Test created by Nobel Laureate Clive Granger holds that media coverage causes more terrorist attacks, and terrorist attacks cause more media coverage

An additional important piece of information which must be added to the "framework" of information surrounding this event comes from the Punjab, Pakistan side.

It appears there may be a very real problem in the northern area of India called Kashmir. There is an ongoing, 600 year old property dispute with Pakistan/Islam over control of Kashmir - which started around 1400AD. Currently, India has decided to build dams on rivers running into Pakistan and (the internet site says) starve the Punjab region of northern Pakistan of water. Because of these actions 15M acres of Pakistani planted crops will die this year. (15M acres is 25K sq miles) If this is true – this is a slow train wreck with both wrecked trains carrying nuclear weapons. Pakistan has decided to run a full scale ongoing terrorist war against the Indian held part of Kashmir.

An Indian businessman says he heard the Mumbai terrorists speak to each other and didn't understand or recognize the language they were speaking. Most Indians would be unfamiliar with the dialect spoken in parts of the Kashmir.

One thing we now know for certain - terrorism in India and Pakistan has many different faces – Hindu, muzlum, British, Kashmir, Pakistani and Indian government sponsored, Maoist, Naxalite backed terrorism in the country's east, and let us not forget organized crime in India.

India's most notorious international organized crime boss is Dawood Ibrahim. He has ties to al-Qaida and many terrorist groups though his international crime ring which has been called the **"D-Gang"** by the Indian press. He stands accused of orchestrating the 1993 terrorist bombings in Mumbai, which killed over 250 innocents. The munitions used in the 1993 terrorist attack were smuggled into Mumbai after they were brought in by boat from the coast - from Pakistan - by Dawood Ibrahim's men. The modus operandi of the munitions entry into 1993 Mumbai is almost **an exact copy of what just has happened in this 2008 Mumbai Massacre**. There have been numerous criminal convictions in the 1993 Mumbai terrorist bombing case. Ibrahim was charged, but never brought to trial, because police could never apprehend him.

All of these terrorist and criminal groups are trying to accomplish the same goal – make money and destabilize and/or collapse the ruling governments of India and Pakistan by slaughtering innocents.

The question before us now is – are these independent terrorist and international criminal organizations now working with each other towards achieving their common goal of destabilization - through assisting each other in mutual heroin and opium trading, training, preparing, and even staging past and future terrorist events? (Yes)

It seems very likely that 6.5 days after the Mumbai event, the 10 to 90 escaped terrorists from Mumbai and/or their organizations, hopped a freighter and went to Greece where they staged a 40 city – multi-country - Molotov cocktail assault on Greece and Europe. This assault will only end with Israel invading the Gaza Strip – which will call these muzlum terrorist "freedom fighters" - back to "Gaza to Get Even".

There are billions of dollars to be made in Mumbai - but - the monetary decisions resulting in political and business acquisitions have their consequences. These consequences or resultant realities must be resolved with the foundation of Hindu life and existence – the "Pure Act".

Only then will the ultra-religious majority of the population in this country be allowed to heal themselves. Perhaps for the time being they might reject terrorism in all forms as a viable political solution to the issues they are currently confronting.

Perhaps the Hindus might discover different ways to interpret and relate to the Bhagavad-Gita – instead of allowing religious extremists to use this holy book as sanctification for terrorism and murder against one's brother. (The "Pure Act" – a man has to do what a man has been born to do)

And let us not forget the Islamic religion. It is so very wrong to interpret "the sharia" – as to religiously justify the mass murder of innocents, be they anyone who doesn't believe in Islam or – murdering Muslims who don't believe in their specific interpretation of "the sharia". Following a mass murder interpretation of "the sharia" takes this religion out of the ranks and definitions of a religion and places this grouping of individuals with this specific mass murder belief defect, into the definition of what I know as a cult – with the followers of this dark cult called muzlumz.

INTRODUCTION

To frame this story - to give someone in the future a sense of what was going on in the USA and world immediately prior to - and immediately after this event – I have included headlines from the world news networks as reported 24 hours prior and 6 days after this event.

Chapter One

The Day Before

November 25, 2008 Tuesday

November 25, 2008 Tuesday

USA news media News Headlines - The Day Before

The Indian Navy mistakenly fired on and sunk a Thailand fishing vessel - thinking the 14 fisherman were pirates. The Indian Navy then left the scene without rendering aid last week - the ship owner said today. All 14 hands are suspected as lost at sea.

Kandahar, Afghanistan - 15 schoolgirls and teachers were burned with acid by the Taliban - for being female and attending school said the Taliban. The acid was shot out of squirt guns and supposedly bankrolled by a rich Pakistani.

US deaths in Afghanistan total 623 today.

Pakistan will receive a $7B loan from the International Monetary Fund to avoid a financial collapse.

Somali pirates have seized another ship off their coast - this time a Yemeni ship. 18 ships have been seized in the last 10 days. The Yemeni ship was carrying steel.

Former driver and body guard of Osama Bin Laden will be moved from Guantanamo to his native Yemen to serve out the rest of his sentence – he could be released in January with credit for time served.

Bush has pardoned 14 and commuted 2 prison sentences.

Gold is over 800 an ounce – 811.0 – up from 770s last week. Pork Bellies 92.10

Pulte Homes will stop paying dividends in the first quarter of 2009 – they were at one time the largest home builder in the US.

Starbucks says they do not project sales to grow in 2009.

Existing home sales drop 3% in October and prices fall more than 11% from a year ago.

In 2007 there were 6M Americans out of work – this year in 2008 there are 9M Americans out of work.

Today gas is $1.55 per gallon retail - in most of Metro-Detroit.

Dow is up to the 8500s – as stocks rally for the 3rd day in a row.

10 % of our seniors live in poverty.
86 % of seniors are stressed by the state of the economy.

Federal Reserve will buy up to $600B in mortgage backed assets in an attempt to ease the financial crisis.

Gold 819.6 at 9AM Central

There have been 172 murders in Washington DC so far this year.

Paulson speaks and no matter what he says the market tanks – down 40 points since he spoke this morning.

Is the President-Elect the President? CNN asks - the markets are reacting to Obama in this fashion.

3M homes in the US will be lost in foreclosure proceedings in the coming year - CNN predicts.

FDIC names 54 new "problem banks" added to their "171 problem bank watch list".

Chapter Two

Immediately Prior

November 26, 2008 Wednesday

Headlines from news agencies world wide immediately prior to the start of the event

November 26, 2008 Wednesday
Immediately Prior

6:30AM Central - "I Was Abducted by Aliens" is the lead 7 to 10 minute news story on CNN– with "more aliens tomorrow on CNN" - and "please send in your UFO photos to CNN" – (honest – I'm not making this up).

A Thailand General calls for elections to end protests after the Bangkok airport is seized by protestors. Also asks protestors to leave Bangkok.

CNN shows more alien spaceship stuff for 10 minutes at 7:30AM Central.

First time jobless claims for last week were at 529K – US government – MSNBC.

AP: Today the Feds have said – The Feds got word in September of a terrorist attack against New York subway system during the holidays.

1 out of 2 houses purchased in California last month were foreclosed houses and priced 40% below the comparable houses in the same area.

Somalia has had no formal government since 1991.

Somalia pirates have seized 39 ships this year.

Gold is at 811.90 an ounce at 9:45AM Central.
DOW is at 8412 at 9:45AM Central.
Oil is at $50 even at 9:45AM Central.

Chapter Three

IN THE BEGINNING
A SITE AND EVENT OVERVIEW

IN THE BEGINNING – A SITE OVERVIEW
November 26, 2008 Wednesday

A slight background on the physical city of Mumbai originally known as Bombay until 1991- it has an urban population of 13.7M with an additional 7M in the metro area. It is a large island very close to the coast of mainland India. Mumbai has many tributaries and the Ulhas River at its island's northern boundary. The island is surrounded by Bombay Harbor on the east side and the Arabian Sea on the south and west side - there are lots of waterfront property belonging to this island/city.

Potential Escape Routes: Inside this island city you will find the Sahjay Gandhi National Park. This park is 104 Square Km – or about 50 square miles – or about 7 miles by 7 miles of park to get lost in. I would guess this would be very similar to having an extremely large Central Park in the middle of New York City – that is the size of New York City. This park appears to hold almost 20% of the land belonging to the island city of Mumbai – this is a great place to hide.

East of the main city/island and Bombay Harbor….on the mainland - is a "metro" part of the city called Navi Mumbai. The terrorists could have crossed over one of the Bombay Harbor bridges, probably the one closest to their original insertion point near the landmark Gateway to India – and then could have used The Scion Panvel Highway Bridge– to get to this eastern and separate part of the city to initiate an escape.

In this part of the city – Navi Mumbai – off the main island – on the mainland - is another large acreage "park" called – "open mixed jungle" and "dense mixed jungle". This jungle runs the – almost 10 mile - length of Navi Mumbai. This could be used as an escape route that runs to the north of India by land. Or this strip of jungle could be used to get to the water on the south side of the city - right up to the waterfront on the eastern side of Bombay Harbor. The route sneaks by Ayyappa airport in the jungle. Why not go inside the airport and fly out of town? If not – after you sneak by the airport you could easily escape by water which is very close by or get picked up on the Scion Panvel Highway which winds by the "dense jungle"/waterfront – at the end of the "jungle escape route" – next to Bombay Harbor. This would be my escape route. Then perhaps to an island near the island park called Elephanta Islands – and from there to the ocean.

The terrorists left their boats where they could easily be found by authorities. Perhaps they had another water based escape route with other boats stashed somewhere. Why did they devise a plan that would leave 2 to 4 rubberized boats where they were found? Why devise a plan that leaves explosives where they were found? (Are there 2-3 or 4 rubberized boats?)

Back to the event: One of the other terrorist teams probably took the Eastern Express Highway to their northern Mumbai Island targets. Leaving the two to four - "hotel room check in" - teams at their hotel rooms at the Taj Mahal and the Oberio Hotels – where they could go out and shoot up a target of opportunity – like the restaurant target - and then get back into the Taj Mahal or some local apartment to reload and take a break.

The 105-year-old Taj Mahal Hotel was built by a Parsi businessman because he was turned away from another hotel for being Indian. The Taj Mahal Hotel is to Mumbai what the Empire State Building is to New York and the Eiffel Tower is to Paris. The Taj Mahal is featured constantly in cinematic films shot by India's movie industry.

The terrorists had ammunition to fire automatic weapons for 3 days – this was an enormous amount of ammo - 10s of thousands of rounds and many clips. If a single terrorist fired 200 rounds per hour for 60 hours (which is a small amount fired in an automatic weapon) – the terrorists would need 12K rounds each. Perhaps they had multiple hotel rooms at the Taj Mahal.

Where the terrorists came ashore they had 3 immediate targets of opportunity – which they did not shoot or blow up - which tells us as much about whom they are as their hard targets.

The Mumbai Massacre Terrorists could have attacked:
The "High Court" -
Mumbai University -
The famous landmark structure called "The Gateway of India" on the waterfront -

Then there were all sorts of Bombay Harbor targets which were available but they only attack one - The Mazagaon Docks, one of India's largest ship-building sites

There were still available as targets of opportunity:
The bridges across the Bombay Harbor -
The 4 airports -
The Prince of Whales Museum - priceless art objects and artifacts -
Bangaga – holiest site in the city -

But the terrorists choose to shoot up very specific targets with a specific message for all of us.

And now for the terrorists trip from Pakistan to Mumbai – which is a little complicated – but as told to us by the captured terrorist Kasab:

The story starts in Muridke, near Lahore, on September 15, as the terrorists travel in groups of two to Karachi. They are ready to leave Karachi on September 27.

From Karachi, Pakistan at 4:15 a.m. on November 23, Kasab – the captured terrorist and his friend Ismail - rowed out to sea along with four other terrorist teams of 2 men each: men Kasab knew as Abu Akasha and Abu Umar; 'Bada' [Big] Abdul Rehman and Abu Ali; 'Chhota' [small] Abdul Rehman and Afadullah; Shoaib and Umar.

They leave from an isolated beach near Karachi in a small boat – unarmed. They are picked up the following day by a larger vessel. At this point they were each given eight hand grenades, an AK-47 rifle, an automatic pistol and 200 rounds of ammunition. In anticipation of a lengthy event, they are also given dried fruit, bags of almonds, steroids, cocaine and LSD.

Interesting point needing to be made – 200 rounds won't last 200 minutes – let alone three days. I could fire 200 rounds at the terrorists in about 5 minutes – given time for reloading. Where did the extra ammo come from? I would need thousands of rounds per hour and hearing protection. I think the 200 rounds were only to be used to protect the terrorists from the boat to where they made contact with the rest of the team at some apartment or hotel room in Mumbai.

When this Pakistan ship gets near the maritime boundary between Pakistan and India - the terrorists then hijacked the Kuber – an Indian fishing trawler. The crew of the Kuber is murdered. (Four of its crew are still missing while the fifth has been found dead, apparently beheaded. Its owner and his brother are being questioned by police.)

On November 23, after reaching Porbandar in the Indian state of Gujarat, 310 nautical miles from Mumbai, the terrorists are intercepted by two coast guard officers. The terrorists hoist a white flag and allow the two coast guard officers to board their boat.

One of the terrorists then attacked and murdered one of the coast guard officers, slitting his throat and throwing him overboard. The other coast guard officer is then forced to help the terrorists reach their destination before being executed as the vessel got near to Mumbai.

Kasab's friend, 25-year-old Abu Ismail, a trained sailor, steered the vessel using GPS equipment.

Three speedboats will meet the Kuber a mile and a half from the Mumbai seafront on Wednesday. (Are these the water taxis now said to have been used during this event?) After waiting for the light to fade, they moved off the Kuber, into the speedboats then later transferring to two inflatable dinghies to row to shore.

Somewhere in the story - is the use of a water taxi owned by an Indian National living in Mumbai. This water taxi is used for transporting terrorists – somewhere - at some point - during the event. Perhaps this is the "speedboat" that takes the terrorists from the fishing vessel Kuber to a point where the rubber dinghies are used to row into shore.

(Conflicting information coming up) Upon reaching Mumbai, they rowed the last few nautical miles to Budhwar Park in 2 to 4 inflatable dinghies. From their first landfall in Budhwar Park, they traveled to their targets by hailing taxis – leaving bombs in the taxis - which will blow up after the terrorists have reached their destination and left these vehicles.

Each man was equipped with a Kalashnikov rifle and 200 rounds of ammunition and grenades. The group also had at least one state-of-the art Garmin global positioning system, and several mobile phones fitted with SIM cards, which have now been determined to have been purchased in Kolkata and New Delhi. Three of the men had larger bags, packed with five timer-controlled Improvised Explosive Devices.

The five – two man teams - then split up. Four terrorists went to the Taj Mahal Hotel, two to the Jewish Community Center - The Chabad House/Nariman House, Kasab and another man set off by taxi towards the railway station, and two terrorists headed for the Café Leopold restaurant.

To contradict Kasab's story slightly at this point– or add to it – we know there were 4 terrorists at the train station murdering the passengers – not 2 or 3 terrorist as Kasab says in his interrogation.

While the other terrorist teams were executing hostages at the Taj Mahal, Kasab and Ismail first opened fire with their assault rifles at around 10:20 PM, killing dozens of people standing at Chhatrapati Shivaji railway station, said Kasab.

The terrorist's first attack – that no one wants to discuss - will be on a police station – the police are murdered and the terrorists put on their uniforms. Immediately following or perhaps during the police station assault - the head of the anti-terrorism unit, the Mumbai chief of police and the head of the anti-corruption unit will be killed in a firefight at a hospital hostage situation. This occurs at about the same time the train station is attacked by 4 terrorists.

Then, the terrorists will visit their co-conspirators who have rented rooms in the Taj Mahal and the Oberoi hotels - and it is believed there is also a rented apartment – to reload their weapons.

The event has started that will last 60 hours over 3 days. After 60 hours – after they run out of ammunition - those terrorists who are not killed escape into crowds forming in the streets.

At one time the government says there are 40 terrorists. Eyewitnesses say there were at least a hundred terrorists leaving the insertion point at Budhwar Park.

Uniformed policemen will refuse to fire their weapons to protect themselves or the many murdered citizens at the train station. Instead the uniformed policemen are also shot and some retreat across the street from the train station.

Having some religious back ground – I would say this is a strict Hindu religious "concept". Strict believers in the Hindu religion will not kill a bee, spider or ant in their house – let alone another human being. I can't bring myself to say the police didn't have the courage to shoot at the terrorists as I just personally don't believe courage entered into this equation – but of course – I could be wrong. But, a future solution would be to only allow followers of the Sikh religion to "Serve and Protect" as they do not have the religious restrictions in their dogma on taking human life to save another life.

Regarding targets, why choose hotels? In the Islamic tradition, when a Muslim invites someone into his home as a guest, this Muslim must protect this invited guest with his life or be dishonored. To someone thinking in another religious or "western" tradition, this will probably be a hard concept to understand. So, why choose a hotel as your target? To show to all Muslims that you as the hotel owner and your society have no honor. This concept, the fact that you have no honor, has much power to those believing in the Muslim tradition. You with no honor deserve to be eliminated.

The captured terrorist told interrogators that the teams remained in touch with the Lashkar headquarters throughout the attack – using their phones through a voice-over-internet service.

The government's response to the terrorist attack will be weak and the event will go on and on for days.

The ongoing and the final death toll numbers could be greatly under reported as could the number of terrorists involved.

The more terrorists the government reports that were involved – then the more terrorists will have had to have escaped - as only 9 terrorists are reported killed and 1 captured.

Another theory about under reporting the count of captured terrorists is that you may be encouraging another ensuing terrorist attack - asking for the release of the captured terrorists. This occurred against India in the recent past, (someone hijacked a jet and demanded the release of the 2006 bomber terrorists who were in custody by the Indian government – which the government capitulated to). It probably didn't occur to the government forces that they shouldn't claim they captured anyone until the end of the event. Now the government says there is only one captured living terrorist from a terrorist group of 10 total. (who somehow staged 10 simultaneous gun battles in 10 separate locations)

CHAPTER FOUR

ZERO HOUR – THE EVENT BEGINS

November 26, 2008 Wednesday
9:30 AM Central – DAY I

Zero Hour – the start

Muzlum terrorists land on the city/island of Mumbai (formally called Bombay) using 2-3 or perhaps 4 boats and attack 10 sites simultaneously (all within an hour or so), using automatic weapons and hand grenades.

The event begins at about 9:30 p.m. local Mumbai time.

The first target is a police station and a hospital - where the head of the anti-terrorism unit, the head of the anti-corruption unit and the chief of police are murdered in a firefight.

After attacking the police station and murdering 14 policemen and the hospital - the terrorists attack the busiest railroad station in Mumbai – at about 10:20 PM. The building is a beautiful example of 19th century Victorian Gothic architecture and is named the Chhatrapati Shivaji railroad station.

The eyewitness who took the now famous photographs of the terrorist shown around the world is Sebastian D'Souza. Mr. D'Souza is a photo editor at the Mumbai Mirror, which is located across the street from the Chhatrapati Shivaji Railway Station. He heard the gunfire, grabbed a camera with a telephoto lens and ran across the street to the railway station to try to take a photo.

By the time he managed to take the now historic photographs of a terrorist, Mr. D'Souza had already watched two terrorists walking across the railway station concourse killing both civilians and policemen. "Many policemen were armed but did not return fire - there were masses of armed police hiding in the area who simply refused to shoot back" he said.

The now historic photo shows a young terrorist — dressed like a college student in cargo pants and a black T-shirt — walking casually through the station, an assault rifle hanging from one hand and two knapsacks slung over a shoulder.

"I first saw the terrorists outside the station," Mr. D'Souza said. "With their rucksacks and Western clothes they looked like backpackers, not terrorists, but they were very heavily armed and clearly knew how to use their weapons."

"There were armed policemen hiding all around the station but none of them did anything," he said. "At one point, I ran up to them and told them to use their weapons. I said, 'Shoot them, they're sitting ducks!' but they just didn't shoot back."

As the terrorists fired at policemen taking cover across the street, Mr. D'Souza realized a train was pulling into the station unaware of the horror occurring inside the train station. "I couldn't believe it. When the train pulled into the station - we rushed to the platform and told everyone to head towards the back of the station. Those who were older and couldn't run, we told them to stay put."

The terrorists returned inside the station and headed towards a rear exit towards Chowpatty Beach.

Mr. D'Souza added: "I told some policemen the terrorists had moved towards the rear of the station but they refused to follow them. What is the point of having policemen with guns if they refuse to use them? I only wish I had a gun rather than a camera."

One terrorist was killed when a policeman at the site returned fire, braving grenades thrown at him. At the same time Kasab, the terrorist in custody, was injured here.

Nasim Inam, another witness to this attack said four of the terrorists gunned down hundreds of commuters. "They just fired randomly at people and then ran away. In seconds, dozens of people fell to the ground bleeding and screaming in pain."

Closed Circuit TV footage from the train station shows that - the Mumbai's police force was hopelessly outgunned and overwhelmed from the attack's earliest moments.

From the closed circuit TV footage - two policemen are seen hiding in an alcove inside the train station as two heavily armed terrorists stalk an empty concourse that just moments before had been crowded with passengers.

One policeman appears to try to take a shot at the terrorists with his ancient Lee Enfield-type bolt-action rifle. He is forced to take cover as one of the terrorists fires an assault rifle from the hip in his direction and a bullet slams into a pillar close to the policeman's head.

During the next two hours, there is an attack every 15 minutes. The attacks start at the police station and hospital followed by the attack on the train station, the Taj Mahal Hotel, the Oberoi Hotel, the Jewish Community Center, a tourist restaurant, The Café Leopold , and two attacks on 2 hospitals. One is a children's hospital - and the other shooting was at a hospital where some of the victims were caught up in the terrorist attack for a second time. Somewhere in the timeline the shipbuilding docks on Bombay Harbor and 2 taxis are bombed and patrons in a movie theater are murdered in their seats later in the event. There were 10 primary targets and many targets of opportunity.

As one team attacked the Taj Mahal – it would appear – at about the same time - the train station is attacked. Another small team of terrorists then attacked anyone they encountered as they walked or drove from the Taj Mahal Hotel, to attack other targets of opportunity inside Mumbai. So, the terrorists have divided into about 7 to 10 teams of about 1 to 4 terrorists each as they attempt to conduct 7 to 10 ongoing gun battles simultaneously. (This is never made clear and will always remain a point of contention)

11AM Central - One hour and 30 minutes into the event - Shooting breaks out near The Times of India newspaper, followed by attacks near the Bombay Municipal Corporation, and The Cama and The GT hospitals. The Jewish Community Center Nariman/Chabad House has been seized by the terrorists.

11:30AM Central – exactly 2 hours into the event - Police say seven sites are under attack. The death toll rises to four – but really is already well over the 100 mark.

The lobbies of both the Oberoi and Taj Mahal hotels are on fire.

Police now surround the Taj Mahal, but no one knows what's going on inside. What is going on inside is wholesale murder, as the terrorists walk through the hotel firing automatic weapons and throwing hand grenades at anything that moved.

12:01PM Central – 12:01 AM local India – Thursday morning Reuters reports: "At least 10 people are killed in Mumbai shootings by terrorists" (the death toll is over 100 at this point)

A car bomb goes off near the city airport. Explosions are heard at the Taj Mahal, and grenades are thrown from the Taj Mahal's windows to the street below.

Guests not held by the gunmen are huddling for shelter where they can inside the sites under siege.

12:30PM Wednesday Central – 12:30 AM Thursday in India – hour 3 of the event -
A British guest escapes from the Taj Mahal and tells Indian television that gunmen are taking hostages and looking for people carrying British and American passports to execute.

The exact time the security forces start entering the Taj Mahal is not clear but it is believed some Indian security forces start to enter the hotel about 3 to 5 hours after the event begins.

When the security forces first enter the hotel they are led around by hotel employees. The only idea they have about what lies ahead is that the "bad guys" have automatic weapons and explosives.

From an interview with an Indian security force commando, "Then we heard gunshots on the second floor and we rushed toward the fired shots," he said. "While taking cover we found that there were 30 to 50 bodies lying dead. At that point we also came under fire. The moment they saw us, they hurled grenades."

The Taj Mahal's enormous atrium and large dome make the sounds of gunfire and explosions endlessly reverberate. It is impossible for the security forces to pinpoint what direction the gunfire is originating from.

01:00PM Wednesday Central – 01:00 AM Thursday in India -
Reuters: At least 18 people killed in Mumbai attacks – from the local Indian TV stations.

Guests and staff are still trying to escape from the two hotels.

A German media executive dies in a fall from the front of the Taj Mahal - trying to climb out a window to get out of the building.

From outside the hotel, people can be seen silhouetted against windows. Some raise their fists vainly against the glass; others flick their lights on and off in distress. A couple take turns waving a white flag.

01:10PM Wednesday Central – 01:10 AM Thursday in India - From Reuters: "At least 40 people are killed in series of attacks in Mumbai – from the local Indian TV channels."

01:30PM Central Wednesday – 01:30 AM Thursday in India - Reuters: "At least 80 killed in Mumbai attacks."

Hemant Karkare, chief of Mumbai's anti-terrorist squad, is now reported to have been murdered early in this event.

"Four or five" terrorists have now taken an unknown number of guests hostage in the two hotels.

At the Taj Mahal there are 50 Korean hostages.

Shortly afterwards, there is an explosion at the Taj Mahal.

02:30 PM Central Wednesday – 02:30 AM Thursday in India- In the Taj Mahal, 20 people hiding in a library area escape with the aid of security forces with a terrorist hiding among them. Businessman Hugh Brown, later says, "When he got out with us, he started shooting some of the people as they were leaving the room. He was then dealt with by the security forces. He pretended to be one of us in the room. He had a rucksack which he wouldn't allow us to look into. He said it was private property. In retrospect, we probably should have done something."

Deccan Mujahideen takes responsibility in emails to press but suspects captured confess to being involved with the Pakistani Lashkar group. Strangely – this email comes to the press via Russia.

03:00 PM Central – 03:00 AM Mumbai
On the TV networks in Mumbai the federal home minister, Shivraj Patil, announces (to the world and the terrorists watching TV) that 200 commandos had taken off on the two-hour flight from New Delhi at 2:30 AM. Even thought the flight is only 2 hours they will not arrive at the scene of the attacks until 06:30AM – 4 hours after they leave for Mumbai. When they arrive it will take hours more to prep them with maps and information - to assist them in their assault to take back 3 held targets.

04:00 PM Central Wednesday – 04:00 AM Thursday India - Immediately after the first moments of the attack, India's elite National Security Guard was dispatched from New Delhi. They arrived in Mumbai at 4am – 7 hours after the start of the event. By 7:00 AM they will have command posts around Nariman House/The Chabad House. They are wearing black jumpsuits with balaclavas, are carrying large bow knives, Glock pistols and submachine guns.

04:30 PM Central Wednesday – 04:30 AM Thursday India - More explosions are reported from the Oberoi Hotel.

Terrorists are "still" throwing grenades from the roof of the Taj Mahal to stop police from entering the hotel.

Hundreds of guests have now been evacuated from the Taj Mahal Hotel, but others, are still held hostage inside. Others are trapped and hiding in their hotel rooms but not captured. Some are crying for help from windows. Firefighters on large ladder trucks are breaking windows to reach them – risking their lives as the event is far from over.

05:45 PM Central Wednesday – 05:45 AM Thursday in India- Officials report 11 police have so far been killed. It is not clear if they are part of the death toll of 80. But then, nothing is clear at this time.

26 of the 50 Koreans who had been trapped in the Taj Mahal are reported to have escaped unharmed. They hid together for five hours in a conference room. No news of what happen to the other 24 Koreans is ever reported.

06:15 PM Central Wednesday – 06:15 AM Thursday in India- The death toll rises to a "reported" 82. An hour later it will reach 86.

In the Taj Mahal, on the 15th floor, security forces are escorting hotel guests out of the hotel. But, the hotel is not under control at this point as firefights between security forces and terrorists will go on at this location for about another 48 hours.

06:30 PM Central Wednesday – 06:30 AM Thursday - Indian Commandoes arrive at the scene in Mumbai – 9 hours after the start of the event and will still need a couple of more hours to gain tactical information on the sites under attack.

07:00 PM Central Wednesday – 07:00 AM Thursday in India- As the sun comes up, the Taj Mahal is surrounded by armed police, ambulances, and fire engines. Periodic firing is heard, and flames and smoke still escape from the roof.

At the Oberoi Hotel, friends of those trapped inside start to gather in the streets.

09:05 PM Central Wednesday – 09:05 AM Thursday in India-
The terrorists have been caught on video tape by CNN driving
police vehicles through the night and firing automatic weapons
at citizens on the street – 3 are murdered.

The first reports come in that an Israeli Rabbi, his wife and two
children are being held hostage at the Jewish Community
Center – a.k.a. The Chabad House. But – they have been held
captive since hour 1 of this event.

This is the Mumbai headquarters of an ultra-Orthodox Jewish
outreach group. The house serves as an educational center, a
synagogue and offers drug prevention services.

Other families also live at the house which is large, multi-
storied (I believe 5 stories) and appears to be constructed of
cement and brick.

"It seems that the terrorists commandeered a police vehicle
which allowed them easy access to the area of the Chabad
house and they then threw a grenade at a gas pump nearby,"
said Rabbi Zalman Shmotkin, a spokesman for the Lubavitch
movement in New York, adding the attackers then "stormed the
Chabad house." (Kasab confessed to blowing up a gas pump)

Residents tried to protect the Jewish center, clashing with the
gunmen and throwing rocks at them in an effort to drive the
terrorists away, said Puran Doshi, a local businessman who
lives nearby. The crowd eventually retreated under fire from the
terrorists, who threw several grenades, wounding one man and
murdering three others he said. "They fired indiscriminately
into the crowd," Doshi said.

Sanjay Bhasme, 40, who lives in the building behind Chabad
house, said he notified the police after the shooting began about

9:45 p.m., but no police arrived for more than 30 minutes —
and only after he'd repeatedly telephoned for help.

09:30 PM Central Wednesday – 09:30 AM Thursday in India -
A terrorist calling himself Sahadullah calls Indian television
and says: "There are seven of us inside the Oberoi. We want all
Mujahideens held in India released and only after that will we
release the people. Release all the Mujahideens, and Muslims
living in India should not be troubled."

09:30 PM Central Wednesday - 09:30 AM Thursday Mumbai,
India time

This event started 12 hours ago.

State Home Secretary Bipin Shrimali said four suspects had
been killed in two incidents in Mumbai when they tried to flee
in cars.

An auto had reportedly discharged a weapon at the Mumbai
International Airport.

Anti Terrorism Squad member Roy said four more gunmen
were killed at the Taj Mahal.

State Home Minister R.R. Patil said nine more terrorists were
arrested. They declined to provide any further details.

There is a body count which grows constantly throughout the
event as more information is known – the final murder toll is:

300 are injured
200 are murdered
  14 policemen are counted as dead immediately
   11 terrorists are dead – was reduced to 9 dead
    9 terrorists are captured – was reduced to 1 captured

3 suspected terrorists are being held – down to 1
5 terrorists at large – if there were 26 total terrorists

The terrorists are currently holding hostages in some of the hotels.

The Taj Mahal Hotel caught fire and is burning out of control at this moment.

It has been impossible to get more than a brief explanation on this event – even from eye witnesses – as the eye witness only sees a small part of this large event now being called the Mumbai Massacre.

10:00 PM Central - the 12.5 hour mark of the event.

While CNN was showing live footage of the event and getting live interviews outside the Taj Mahal- FOX news was holding a 30 minute anti-Democratic, faux-comedic, right wing piece - between an abrasive Irishman and an old man from Saturday Night Live. FOX news decided not to carry this terrorist event while the event was breaking news.

Indian citizens in the street are very angry over this event and appear almost ready to riot – but that is my opinion. The "citizens on the street" are screaming at Indian reporters from CNN and cannot talk rationally to the reporters on the scene – as they are so excited/angry.

11:40 PM Central Wednesday – 11:40 AM Thursday in India - Confused reports come in from the government.

A state official says "police and commandos have begun operations against the terrorists at the Oberoi but there could still be 100-200 guests and staff trapped there.

02:30PM Central.
The story breaks on cable news in the U.S.. Different cable news stations have different injury and body count numbers at this time.

No more news updates until the next morning in the U.S.

Chapter Five

November 27, 2008 Thanksgiving Thursday

November 27, 2008 Thanksgiving Thursday

12:01 AM Central Thursday – 12:01 PM Thursday in India –

At the Jewish Community Center, a woman, the family's cook and nanny, and a child – Moshe Holtzberg, aged two – escape.

After being shot at she hides in a closet on the first floor for 12 hours listening to continuous gunfire and explosions. The nanny hears the child cry and leaves the closet on the first floor. She goes up to the second floor and finds the baby between the unconscious parents, picks up the baby and escapes the building as automatic gunfire still rages inside the building.

Moshe's trousers are covered in blood and he has a handprint on his back where he was struck so hard he was rendered unconscious for 12 hours. He is now an orphan. His mother and father, Rabbi Gavriel Holtzberg, are later found to have been tortured then murdered inside the house.

01:00 AM Central Thursday – 13:00 PM Thursday in India – Three people are killed in an explosion in a taxi on the Mazagaon Dockyard Road in south Mumbai.

A movie theater, the Metro Adlabs Multiplex, is reported to have been attacked with patrons murdered in their seats.

02:00 AM Central Thursday – 14:00 PM Thursday in India – State Police Chief Roy says the Taj Mahal hostages have all been released. This is not the case.

04:00 AM Central Thursday – 16:00 PM Thursday in India – About a dozen hostages leave the Taj Mahal and climb into ambulances. Three bodies, covered in white sheets, are wheeled out of the hotel.

At the Jewish Community Center 30 more commandos joined police officers in the street – while the Elite special forces team is already on site watching from neighboring roof tops, (with press standing next to them chatting during this ongoing event)

05:00 AM Central Thursday – 17:00 PM Thursday in India – Gunfire and explosions are heard at the Taj Mahal as security teams launch an assault on the terrorists.

06:00 AM Central Thursday – 18:00 PM Thursday in India – At the Chabad House, a gunman calling himself "Imran" calls Indian media and says, in the Urdu dialect: "Ask the government to talk to us and we will release the hostages. Are you aware how many people have been killed in Kashmir? Are you aware how your army has killed Muslims? Are you aware how many of them have been killed in Kashmir this week?"

08:00 AM Central Thursday – 20:00 PM Thursday in India – Huge flames shoot from an upper floor of the Oberoi. Commandos are reportedly fighting room-to-room battles with terrorists.

Half an hour later, 45 hostages are reported freed from the Oberoi, but 35 remain inside.

09:00 AM Central –
There are over 100 hostages still being held with gunfire still erupting across the city.

Released by the government - there are 125 murdered with an additional 200 injured due to the attacks, (the number climbs every hour).

There are believed to be approximately 5 muzlum terrorists still fighting at this time.

Another explosion just occurred at the Taj Mahal Hotel - rated by Forbes magazine as one of the most luxurious hotels in the world.

The Oberio Hotel is currently on fire.

09:30 AM Central –
Approximately 24 hours after the start of the terrorist attacks - the city of Mumbai, India is still under attack.

Information on the event is still very brief with CNN being told repeatedly over the last 12 hours that the event was over and contained – when it obviously was not contained.

In the US - rather than carrying the news/facts as they are happening - FOX news at 24 hours after the start of the event wants to draw illogical conclusions and talk about the event before the facts are even in - even before they have broadcast the facts and of course before this event it even over.

A Rabbi is currently being held hostage sat the Jewish Community Center.

10:00 AM Central Thursday – 22:00 PM Thursday in India – Death toll rises to 119. It is now known that 10 of the dead were murdered at the railway station – this official count at the railway station grows to 45 after the event. Eyewitnesses and even the captured terrorist say the passengers at the railway station were "murdered by the dozens" – "mowed down in seconds".

11:30 AM Central Thursday – 23:30 PM Thursday in India – Again - State officials say the siege at the Taj Mahal has ended and the last three terrorists have been killed. Unfortunately this is the third time this will be announced and it will be said two more times before it becomes a true statement.

Dipak Dutta, rescued from the Taj Mahal, tells how troops escorting him through the corridors told him not to look down at any of the bodies. "Many chef trainees were massacred in the kitchen – there was blood everywhere" he adds.

Eight more hostages are freed from Chabad House.

Two loud explosions and gunfire are heard at the Taj Mahal. Electricity is cut off from the floors where it is believed gunmen still roam.

No new information on the event for 6 hours – everyone in the news business had to eat their thanksgiving turkeys.

05:30 PM Central – hour 32 –
Explosions are still rocking the streets of Mumbai.

The terrorists are holding hostages at the Jewish Community Center and the Oberoi Hotel.

It is looking as though at least one of the 9 dead terrorists is a dead Pakistani. (In July 2006 trains in Mumbai were blown up during rush hour by the Pakistani Lashkar terrorist group killing over 200.)

The terrorists purposely planned and targeted the heads of the Mumbai Police/Security force for assignation to start off the operation.

Chopra and Indian author says: "USA policies perpetuate these attacks – India must ask Pakistan for help in ending this "muzlum extremist group - world uprising".

At 8:45 PM Central –
We now know that 3 of the suspects in custody have admitted they are members of the Pakistani Lashkar Terrorist Group.

CNN and FOX News are featuring news segments on "Heroes" and Conspiracy Theory's - instead of covering the event.

9:00 PM Central - hour 36.5 –
Supposedly the Taj Mahal Hotel has been "cleared" of terrorists (again for the forth time).

Security forces are now going door to door in the Oberoi hotel and have also entered the Jewish Community Center.

It is now reported that 2 Americans have been murdered at The Café Leopold during the opening hour.

The Indian government says "The situation in Mumbai is still not under control" as the event rages on.

09:35 PM Central – hour 36 –
No live coverage from 5 different national cable news services. No information until 12:30AM Central tomorrow. CNN is showing Heroes for hours and hours and FOX shows Hannity and his Conspiracy show and the Palin interview and then the September Obama interview – over and over again while a live terrorist event of historic proportions is ongoing in the world

India's navy claims they stopped a cargo vessel off the coast of India - that could have been the "mother ship" coordinating the attack on Mumbai – releasing the 3 speedboats that landed at the Taj and started this event.

07:00 PM Central – Day II – hour 33.5 –
A boat loaded with explosives is found near the Taj Mahal waterfront. Indian media shows pictures of rubber dinghies found by the city's Bombay Harbor shoreline, apparently used by the terrorists to reach the shore.

Fox news wants to show the old Obama interview by an abrasive Irishman while CNN is covering the event live.

An Israeli extraction team of 8 are headed to Mumbai – they left Israel Thursday afternoon. 2 more explosions are heard.

Indian Black Flag Commandoes are going door to door.

The Indian Prime Minister has just said the terrorists have external links.

It is now believed there are 26 terrorists involved in the event.

It is reported that also killed are the Mumbai Chief of Police, the head of the Anti-Terrorist Unit and the head of the Anti-Corruption Unit. The circumstances surrounding the 14 dead policeman has not yet been mentioned on the news media yet – other than they have been murdered.

During a terrorist event – the best practice is to isolate the recently released hostages to insure that a terrorist doesn't escape posing as an innocent. It looks as though these terrorists could have escaped by placing down their weapons and posing as regular citizens – and just walking into the crowds on the streets.

During this event the police did not have enough control of this event to isolate released hostages. This citywide attack event was way too large for an unprepared and unsuspecting security force. The crowds have not been prevented from gathering outside the hotels and other targets.

New weapons firing is currently going off within the Taj Mahal Hotel, Oberoi Hotel and the Jewish Community Center.

07:30 PM Central – Day II - hour 34 –
There are at least 3 simultaneous hostage situations are ongoing in the city of Mumbai.

Security forces have landed on the roof of the Jewish Community Center via a helicopter and CNN has a live feed of this assault – I hope the terrorists aren't watching the assault on TV as I am at the moment. I could hear a live conversation by 3 commandoes outside the Jewish Center – which was captured and fed to the US-CNN.

An Indian commando team rappels from helicopters during the insertion into the Jewish Community Center and then a large explosion rocks the building and blows a gaping hole in the wall.

Unfortunately we will later discover that all 5 hostages have been tortured and murdered prior to or perhaps during this insertion. The Chabad House name is getting co-mingled with the name Nariman House – we are given 2 Jewish Community Center names. Later it will be determined that the Nariman House is located next door to the Chabad house and that a terrorist was seen jumping from the roof of the Chabad House to the Nariman House – taking the fight from the Chabad House to the Nariman House.

Once the commandoes enter the Jewish Center - CNN should have a good live feed of this event. Unfortunately CNN has now switched to their "Heroes" program naming their "Heroes" of the year – so there will be no live feed of the Jewish Center assault.

It is not known at this time but the battle for the Jewish Community Center will go on for about 12 hours – after the helicopter lands the commandoes on the roof.

The Jewish Community Center is run by the ultra-orthodox Jewish outreach group Chabad Lubavitch.

Indian army snipers in buildings opposite the Jewish Community Center – Chabad/Nariman House open fire. Then commandos rope down from a hovering helicopter on to the roof of the Jewish Community Center enter.

Associated Press: This insertion "was punctuated by gunshots and explosions - and at one point an intense exchange of fire that lasted several minutes - as forces cleared it floor by floor".

By Friday afternoon, the security forces had control of the top two floors.

Just after dusk, a massive explosion shook the Jewish Community Center, blowing out windows in neighboring buildings. Gunfire and smaller explosions followed the first blast.

One camouflaged commando came out with a bandage on his forehead, while soldiers fired smoke grenades into the building and a steady stream of gunfire reverberated across narrow alleys.

08:30 PM Central Thursday
No news agency but CNN was covering this event live moment by moment - then at 8:30PM Central CNN ceased live coverage of the event.

10:00 PM Central Thursday – 10:00 AM Friday in India – More guests, including a chef, a baby and people carrying luggage bearing Canadian flags, are led from the Oberoi.

11:30 PM Central Thursday – 11:30 AM Friday in India – A police officer outside the Oberoi shouts through a loudhailer that 93 guests have so far been rescued from the hotel. Almost simultaneously - "on queue" - an explosion goes off inside the hotel.

At the Oberoi, dozens are still being held hostage. An official says security forces have cleared the ground to the fourth floors, and the eighth to the 21st floors.

Chapter Six

November 28, 2008 Friday

November 28, 2008 Friday

12:30 AM Central - hour 38

Two dozen more people are rescued from the Oberoi Hotel. Those rescued are mainly air crews with Lufthansa and Air France.

Half an hour later, a commando officer reports that they have found 15 bodies in a room at the Taj Mahal Hotel.

93 hostages are released/freed from the Oberio Hotel while a large explosion in the street outside of the Taj Mahal occurs during a live CNN interview.

Indian security forces have killed the two last terrorists inside the Oberoi Hotel.

"The Oberoi Hotel is under our control," J.K. Dutt, director general of India's elite National Security Guard (NSG) commando unit, told reporters, adding that 24 bodies had been found.

A 51-year-old from London - describing the scene when he was eventually led to safety - he said it was "carnage" with "blood and guts everywhere". For almost two days, a 51-year-old from London had locked himself in his room to escape the terrorists who were holding hostages several floors below. He spent his time listening to gunshots and explosions and communicating with the outside world on his phone and Blackberry. This was after the terrorists went ballistic - killing wildly in the initial raid on the Oberoi Wednesday night. It was very, very upsetting,' he told the BBC. "Just before I went to my room I had had dinner in the Kandahar restaurant. I have now found out that it was one of the restaurants where the terrorist attacks started. Unfortunately, the waitress who served me was one of the first to get murdered." Speaking of his relief, he added: "It is great to be out. It has been 48 hours, but without food and water - surrounded by explosions and gunshots and people running down corridors screaming…. it has been grim, very grim."

It has been reported by the Indian Government News Agency that the terrorists had set up "Control Room Headquarters" in hotel rooms in both the Taj Mahal and the Oberio – "weeks if not months in advance".

FOX is showing the Palin interview again – obviously FOX has no ability to get live video feeds from anywhere that is not in the USA.

CNN on the other hand had employees staying at the Taj Mahal and Oberio whom they were able to interview live. There was also a CNN local reporter, who spoke very good English, on the scene reporting with a camera crew at about the 12 hour mark of the event.

Unfortunately CNN had committed their network to a special night called Heroes – where CNN names everyday heroes from our country. This night's programming on CNN has been advertised for about a month. It is a shame that this nights programming had to conflict with this historic and major news story…..the largest city and financial center in India is taken over by terrorists for 60 hours and almost 500 are murdered or wounded – hostages are taken– and gun battles are raging at 7 to 10 locations - simultaneously.

12:45 AM Central – hour 38.25 –
The Taj Mahal was told it was going to be attacked weeks ago and set up lines of defense around the building. The funny

thing is they were attacked. The attackers were customers renting rooms from the hotel - for use as headquarters during the coming terrorist attack. These customers easily infiltrated the lines of defense set up around the hotel by the Mumbai security forces and walked up to the Taj Mahal Hotel front desk and paid for rooms.

How do you as a hotel - defend against terrorists who are your customers - who have rented rooms from you?

It is now reported that the terrorists left Karachi, Pakistan on Wednesday on a boat headed for Mumbai. There is at least one Pakistani National amongst the terrorists.

01:00 AM Central – hour 38.5 –
CNN is still playing "Heroes" and FOX is playing again for the 3rd time in the last 12 hours – from September – the old Obama and abrasive Irishman interview.

03:00 AM Central Friday – 15:00 PM Friday in India -
Indian police claim to have control of the Oberoi. They have so far recovered 24 bodies.

At Chabad House, commandos soon report they have taken the top two floors in what is dubbed Operation Black Tornado.

The death toll reaches 143, with 288 injured.

However, at the Taj Mahal Hotel, security officers were still battling up to six terrorists believed to be holed up in the ballroom with 200 hostages.

The Indian authorities thought they had ended the siege at the Taj Mahal last night - after they shot three terrorists dead and released hundreds of hostages but battles raged inside the Taj Mahal again today.

04:30 AM Central – 04:30 PM Mumbai -
At the Jewish Community Center - the commandos enter a fifth-floor apartment from the roof and drape a red flag in the window—this is a signal to others on their team. It becomes clear they don't have radios. In order to communicate with each other they either speak to each other in person, use their cell phones or drape red flags in windows.

05:00 AM Central Friday – 17:00 PM Mumbai Friday -
The sniper teams continued shooting into the fourth floor of the Jewish Community Center - through broken glass and curtains.

The commandos fire a succession of rockets into the fourth floor, taking out what little remained of the wall to obscure the view into the building. The building's upper walls are now thoroughly pockmarked with bullet holes and soot-covered from explosions.

Commandos can be seen walking around the first floor, and moving around the stairwell. They lean over the roof and shoot down into the windows. More explosions and small arms fire can be heard.

05:30 AM Central Friday – 17:30 PM Mumbai Friday -
The fourth floor of Chabad/Nariman House explodes shaking all of south Bombay and sending everyone nearby to the ground looking for cover.

A massive explosion is reported from The Chabad House, when commandos blow up an outer wall to gain access to the compound.

Commandos enter the building, emptying machine gun clips in quick succession.

06:00 AM Central Friday – 18:00 PM Friday in India -
Chabad House is still under terrorist control. Commandoes are still on the roof of the Chabad House (a.k.a. the Chabad Center) – 10.5 hours after they were inserted by a helicopter.

There is more shooting at the Taj Mahal as Indian forces begin firing grenades at the Taj Mahal, where at least one gunman is holed up in the ballroom – we will later find out with 200 hostages.

07:00 AM Central Friday – 19:00 PM Friday in India -
At The Chabad House/Nariman House, Indian Security Forces leave, firing their weapons in the air, to signal that at last The Jewish Community Center has been liberated. The bodies of six hostages and two gunmen are found inside. The termination of this situation took 11.5 hours from insertion by helicopter to completion - but came 46.5 hours after the start of the occupation.

Rabbi Gavriel Holtzberg, 29, will be found by his colleague, Rabbi Goldberg, lying slumped on the ground of his living quarters wrapped in tefillin, a prayer aid containing the Hebrew scrolls. On his bedside table is found copies of Jewish holy texts along with a book entitled: "How to protect yourself when terrorists come to your house."

 08:30 AM Central – hour 47 –
There are new developments. Even though the Indian government has announced that the Taj Mahal has been cleared 4 times now – new gunfire has erupted in 2 different places within the Taj Mahal and explosions have been heard.

Also, it is now known that the first site attacked was the Mumbai police station where the terrorists removed the uniforms of the murdered policemen.

The death toll is now at 151 murdered and approximately 300 injured at hour 47 of the event.

Crowds are growing in the streets across from known terrorist sites.

CNN is now saying that the last stronghold of the terrorists is in the Taj Mahal Hotel perhaps in a ballroom.

Gunfire and explosions can be heard outside the Taj Mahal on the street where crowds are growing.

The terrorists must have rented more than 1 room at the Taj Mahal and filled it with terrorists and ammo – perhaps a room on each floor.

Crowds are growing in the streets here also – literally packing the streets – taking control of the streets – so that a vehicle cannot drive through – and the crowds are angry.

It appears that the media is co-mingling the term Chabad House and Nariman House as the Jewish Community Center – as CNN has just announced that 5 hostages and 2 terrorists are dead at the Chabad house – which was the death toll CNN had attached to the Nariman House minutes ago. Later we will find out a terrorist jumped from the Chabad House to the Nariman House and took the fight with him.

Israeli Foreign Minister speaks at press conference – same information again – 5 hostages murdered and 2 terrorists dead at the Jewish Community Center.

Senior US military officials are standing by in case the Indian government requests any military aid to assist in putting down the ongoing event.

Brittan and Israel have sent government advisors to Mumbai and Israel sent commandoes.

At the Taj Mahal 100 more commandos have arrived in military trucks for what is hoped to be the final assault.

Military snipers can be seen on cranes and fire department ladders overlooking the hotel.

10:00 AM Central - Day III – hour 48.5 —
Gunfire is still heard from inside the Taj Mahal Hotel.

The USA is sending investigators to Mumbai. It appears some British nationals were involved in this event.

The Indian Prime Minister has stated that the terrorists came from Pakistan – Pakistan denies involvement.

Both Pakistan and India have nuclear bomb capability.

Again the Indian government says the Oberoi Hotel has been cleared

FOX news is showing the video of the commandoes on the roof or some roof from supposedly a live video feed – I am recognizing this video as the insertion by helicopter onto the roof of the Jewish Community Center from yesterday – this event at the Jewish Community Center has been over for 3 hours at this point.

04:00 PM Central – DAY III – hour 54.5 –
Gunfire and explosions can still be heard from the live CNN camera feed in front of the Taj Mahal.

CNN has no live video feeds or any new information – they only recapitulate what has already been disseminated to the public for the last 48 hours, like FOX News.

CNN's interview with the Pakistan ambassador to the US was very good. Pakistan will work with India to locate the guilty of this event and stop terrorism as terrorists are no one's friends. Pakistan has been the victim of terrorism itself - with the Pakistan President or the Prime Minister having lost his wife to a terrorist attack last year. Pakistan hopes this event will bring the 2 democratic countries closer together as 2 democracies have never fought each other.

The Pakistan Ambassador to the USA - believes there are Al Qaeda links to this event via the modus-operandi.

The Pakistan Ambassador to the US - has unbelievably good command of the English language.

CNN shows the same video clips from 24 hours ago - repeatedly (i.e. from the hospital with the man shot in the shoulder).

05:00 PM central – DAY III - hour 56.5 –
A new firefight at the Taj Mahal Hotel is taking place at this moment – gunfire can be heard on the street.

The local citizens mobbing on the street are already blaming the government for allowing this to go on so long – told to reporters in live CNN street interviews of "citizens of Mumbai on the street".

05:30 PM Central - DAY III – hour 56 –
CNN is now showing a video from hour number 8 – the first video shown is now being shown by CNN as if it were the latest live video feed – the video of the 100 people running from the Taj Mahal after an explosion.

Only old coverage from CNN – no coverage from FOX as only CNN appears to have worldwide coverage.

CNN now showing memorial on the Jewish Rabbi being killed – this has its place after the event – not during

If this event happened in a US city – regular citizens would probably go down to the Taj Mahal Hotel with their own weapons and assist in holding the site and perhaps assist in clearing it.   In 1966 this is exactly what happened during the Texas Tower Event. Charles Whitman murders his family then climbs a large 26 story clock tower on the campus of Texas A&M and starts shooting randomly at people down below – killing 17 and wounding about 30. The local police were outgunned and did not have weapons which could reach the gunman at the top of the tower. Local citizens started driving up in their vehicles and retuning fire with high powered rifles – creating suppressing fire – which limited the shots available to Whitman and also allowed the police to storm the tower and end the event.

06:00 PM Central - Day III – hour 56.5 –
There appears to be plenty of ammunition for the terrorists- as gunfire is still being heard in front of the Taj Mahal.

CNN now has a new – news story - recapping the entire event – interesting – but not anything new.

Finally as I was about to change the channel – away from CNN - 10 seconds perhaps only 5 seconds of live video footage outside the Jewish Community Center is shown – the streets are packed with people chanting and screaming – almost a riot – we would call this a riot in Detroit - the citizens of Mumbai are very mad and screaming in the streets at the moment.

The citizens of Mumbai have so filled the streets in front of the Jewish Community Center– you could not drive a car or any vehicle - through this screaming – chanting - antagonized crowd/mob. (Maybe this is why CNN is not showing any live video footage – Mumbai citizens are rioting in the streets calling for an end to this event)

06:30 PM Central – DAY III – hour 57 –
Gunfire is still erupting out of the Taj Mahal Hotel – there is no end of this event in sight.

07:30 PM Central Friday – 07:30 AM Saturday in India - Hour 58 of DAY III – The Final Assault Is About To Begin

Gunfire is still erupting out of the Taj Mahal Hotel – it appears there is no end of this event in sight – no new video feeds from CNN.

Smoke is billowing from the ground floor of the Taj Mahal.

What is to be the final assault and final battle of this terrorist event begins as Indian Security Forces and terrorists are fighting each other from room to room inside the Taj Mahal.

Three terrorists are killed and finally the body of one terrorist is later thrown from a window onto the street.

Sniffer dogs are led into the hotel to search for bombs and bodies.

08:00 PM Central – The Taj Mahal is still exploding, burning and smoking.

09:00 PM Central Friday – 09:00 AM Saturday in India – During the final assault by commandoes on the Taj Mahal – the security teams find "rooms full of bodies" at the Taj Mahal – as the death toll climbs to 195.

The building has experienced multiple hand grenade explosions and fires throughout the entire structure and many rooms are gutted. The outside of the structure shows signs of fire. It will take a lot of work to put this hotel back the state it was in prior to the attack.

09:30 PM Central Friday – 09:30 AM Saturday in India

The FINAL battle at the Taj Mahal came to an end with a final firefight at a ballroom holding 200 hostages.

No information is ever released on the fate of the 200 hostages in the ballroom – in the last battle.

Police now are saying there were only 10 terrorists - total.

How did 10 simultaneous events occur with only 10 terrorists when they were seen to be working in teams? The earlier government reports said there were between 26 to 40 terrorists – which sound more like the truth. Eyewitnesses to the terrorists arriving in boats in Bombay Harbor said there were over 100 terrorists.

CNN says the end of the event came at hour 60.

A commando revealed he had seen at least 50 bodies littering the Taj hotel floor after Special Forces stormed the building and rescued hundreds of guests. Clad in black, with a mask covering his face, the unit chief said: "There was blood all over the bodies. The bodies were strewn here and there and we had to be careful as we entered the building to avoid further bloodshed of innocent civilians."

Chapter Seven

The Days After

November 29, 2008 Saturday

November 29, 2008 Saturday

We can say that the event probably ended about 60 hours after it started – but this event is really a little longer as the event starts with the terrorists leaving Pakistan. Or we could say it first starts with the murder of the crew of the Indian fishing vessel Kuber.

CNN showed repeats of Larry King and the Heroes special over night at about hour 61-68 of the event. CNN did not cover this event to its conclusion – nor did CNN have any idea when and or how the event ended. Though I am sure there was plenty of live video to chose from – we got nothing from CNN but the same video shots from hour 12 – 24 over and over and over until the end of the event.

09:30AM Central - the end of Day III - and the start of DAY IV – hour 72 –
CNN says the event might be over as the shooting has ceased.

Maybe the terrorists just ran out of bullets after shooting for 3 days straight – their hands aching from firing guns for 3 days – they got hungry – with ears ringing - and went out for breakfast.

They probably simply set down their guns, and then walked out the door. Then they simply melted into the crowds which had gathered outside the target sites in the streets – almost rioting in front of the Jewish Community Center.

10:30 AM Central - hour 73 - one hour into DAY IV –
CNN says that no one is sure or certain this event is over.

New information updates on the event:

The main target was to blow up the Taj Mahal Hotel – the terrorists expected to kill 5K people by blowing up the Taj Mahal - but for unknown reasons the attempt was unsuccessful.

A large amount of explosives were found – actually during the event – near the Taj Mahal Hotel –it was reported early during the event.

Satellite cell phones were found in one of the 3 hijacked landing craft. The terrorists also were using Blackberrys and accessing Google Earth during the event.

Some terrorists probably escaped.

3 Terrorists were killed in the Taj Mahal during the last exchange of gunfire with the Indian commandoes early Saturday morning USA time.

2 PM Central – DAY IV – hour 76.5 into the Mumbai Massacre – CNN again says this may not be over - as the Indian security forces are still going door to door within the Taj Mahal and the Oberio Hotels.

But- shooting or explosions have not been heard in the last 12 hours – except for what has been called purposeful explosions in the Taj Mahal - as Indian security forces set off explosive devices left behind by the terrorists.

November 30, 2008 Sunday

November 30, 2008 Sunday

09:30 AM Central - the end of Day IV - and the start of DAY V – hour 96 -

CNN knew at the start of this event - at hour 12 of 60 - that the terrorists were walking around looking for people with American and British passports to execute.

Very few Americans were murdered during this event – maybe 5 or 8. This might cause one to wonder about whether the purpose of the attack was to execute Americans. This event required a lot of work to stage, for murdering perhaps 10 Americans and Britons. It would appear the terrorists did their homework on staging this event – so, wouldn't the terrorists have known beforehand as they were in the planning stage, that there were going to be few Americans and British deaths as a result of their actions? Of course, so this obviously was not the terrorist's purpose of staging this event.

The murdering of 5K people while blowing up the Taj Mahal Hotel - as the main terrorist goal, sounds plausible.

The purpose of the event looks more like an attempt to destabilize India's commercial district and perhaps India's commercial relations with the international community, while perhaps also raising the international stress level between India and Pakistan.

The more internally destabilized India and Pakistan are - the more vulnerable they both are to internal muzlum extremist seditionary forces and ensuing internal terrorist events targeted against their respective governments.

The new body count is 11 Terrorists were killed – 1 captured alive – and the rest got away – they simply melted into the crowds in the streets. The terrorists didn't even need an escape route. This information of - 11 Terrorists were killed – 1 captured alive - differs radically from the information given to CNN at the 12 hour mark of this event – which was:

11 terrorists are dead – which will be reduced to 9 dead
 9 terrorists are captured – which will be reduced to 1
 3 suspected terrorists are being held in custody – to 1
 5 terrorists are still at large - unknown
26 terrorists total - unknown

India's Home Minister has resigned due to large amounts of negative criticism towards him by the population regarding the way this event was handled by internal Indian Security forces – and it would appear that the Home Minister should have had the country more prepared for terrorists attacks.

The slow response to ending the event by Indian Security forces is in question at the moment – as the event took over 60 hours to be terminated.

India is reported to be moving troops to the Pakistan border. The Pakistan ambassador to the USA says Pakistan is not moving troops to the Indian Boarder.

The Pakistan ambassador to the USA also extends his sorrow to India - that this event has occurred – and he asks India to work as partners with Pakistan to rid both countries of the enemy of all humanity – the terrorists.

The Pakistan ambassador to the USA has announced that Pakistan will cooperate completely in all phases of any investigation into this event and will instigate criminal proceedings against any terrorists found in Pakistan.

There are candlelight vigils in the streets of Mumbai.

The citizens of Mumbai want to know how the event could have lasted so long and what is the Indian government going to do to improve their protection of the population against another attack?

US News has the Indian security forces still going door to door within the Taj Mahal Hotel.

December 1, 2008 Monday

December 1, 2008 Monday

09:30 AM Central - the end of Day V - and the start of DAY VI
– hour 120 -

CNN says the Indian Security forces are still going room to room inside the Taj Mahal.

FBI investigators from the USA have arrived in Mumbai to assist in the investigation.

The final body count - 8 Americans dead in this event.

The Chief Minister of the state of Maharashtra, India where Mumbai is located has resigned. He said he would leave it up to his ruling Congress party to decide whether his resignation would be accepted. His announcement followed Sunday's resignation of The Federal Home Minister who resigned amid criticism of the slow response to the attacks that left 200 dead and 300 wounded.

It is now believed there were 15 terrorists who landed by the 3 boats found near the Gateway to India landmark – based on 15 sets of equipment found at or near the boats.

The US Counterterrorism Department warned India of a possible maritime attack on Mumbai weeks before the attack.

December 2, 2008 Tuesday

December 2, 2008 Tuesday

09:30 AM Central - the end of Day VI - and the start of DAY VII – hour 144 -

India demands that Pakistan captures India's most wanted criminal hiding for the last 15 years in Pakistan and transfer this terrorist to India for trial. This terrorist was the leader of the Mumbai 2002 train bombing event which killed 250.

India is also demanding that Pakistan turn over 20 terrorist wanted in India – one since 1981.

Indian medical experts say that it is very clear that the 6 murdered Jewish hostages from the Chabad house were tortured before they were murdered.

Pakistan and India have fought 3 wars since their separation or partitioning, in 1947.

A passenger train has been blown up by muzlum terrorists in northern India killing 2 and injuring 30.

In Mumbai, India, the local Muslim cemetery refuses to bury the 9 terrorists killed during the event. Islamic custom requires the local Islamic cemetery to accept unclaimed Islamic bodies and to provide a burial function after 3 days.

The local Islamic cemetery has stated that these dead terrorists cannot be followers of Islam after committing the inhuman atrocities and killing of innocent Muslims – and therefore cannot be buried in an Islamic cemetery.

Somalia pirates are holding 300 crew members and about a dozen ships for ransom at the moment.

Italy arrests muzlum terrorists planning event in Milan.

UK – new law will allow police "war powers" - to stop anyone without cause - request ID -and jail for refusal or non-compliance if deemed necessary.

Stay of execution ordered in the case of US soldier Ronald Grey – convicted in 1988 of rape and murder - who was to be executed by lethal injection.

German soldiers in Afghanistan deemed to fat to fight – 40% of 18 to 29 year old German soldiers are overweight– London Times (compared to 35% of the citizen population). German authorities have stated that in 2007 the 3.5K German troops in Afghanistan consumed - 1.7 M pints of beer and 90K bottles of wine (which is 1.5 pints per day and 2 bottles of wine per month per soldier). In contrast US and UK forces in the country have a strict no alcohol policy.

"Ripsaw" a U.S. unmanned tank/machine gun mobile platform - video - is released to the US news media.

Thailand protestors have lifted their 8 day blockade of Bangkok's 2 main airports. Totals are now at 270K stranded tourists trying to leave the country.

Luxury Cruise ship outruns pirates/terrorists - A USA based 30,000-ton luxury cruise ship, the M/S Nautica, outran pirates in two small skiffs firing rife shots at the cruise ship. This happened off the coast of Yemen this weekend, the ship's owner said Monday. The ship was on a 32 day cruise from the Rome to Singapore.

On Sunday, an official from the Kenya Seafarers Association said pirates have reached a deal with the owners of a Ukrainian ship - the MV Faina. The Faina was loaded with Soviet-era tanks, tank artillery shells, grenade launchers and small arms - that were seized on September 25, 2008. The pirates settled for a $20M ransom. The ship was headed for Kenya, whose government bought the weapons from the Ukraine.

From Tuesday
Oil $47 a barrel.
Gold is a 777.90.
LA high of 70F.
Detroit is at 26F.
Yen is at 93.

Obama officially names:
H. Clinton as the Secretary of State
Eric Holder as the Attorney General
Defense Secretary Robert Gates stays in position for a while
Retired Marine Gen. Jim Jones as National Security Adviser
Arizona Gov. Janet Napolitano as Homeland Security Secretary
Susan Rice will be the new Ambassador to the United Nations.

USA bi-partisan think group claims terrorists will use weapons of mass destruction within the USA within the next 5 years – either nuclear or biological – claim that anthrax would be the easiest.

Republicans wins the Georgia 2-way redo of the 3-way November election for a Georgia US Senate seat. This will prevent Democrats from gaining a majority to prevent a "filibuster" by the Republicans.

December 3, 2008 Wednesday

December 3, 2008 Wednesday

09:30 AM Central - the end of Day VII - and the start of DAY VIII – hour 168 since the start and 108 hours since the event was terminated.

Explosive devices in a bag left from the attack were found at the Mumbai main train station and defused. It is unclear why the bomb was not found earlier and why it is now found as the US Secretary of State arrives in India.

Secretary of State Rice has said that Pakistan has pledged this morning they will follow all leads in the investigation - wherever the leads take them.

Pakistan has said they will take criminal action against all conspirators found in Pakistan. Pakistan will not allow extradition to India but will stage trials in Pakistan.

It appears that the Pakistan government is being held hostage itself by internal radical muzlum extremist groups as Pakistan admits to being worried of "backlash" by the muzlum extremists within its boarders.

Pakistan says it is already in an "information sharing" situation with India regarding this event.

The Mumbai Chief of Police has just revealed that they know for sure that the terrorists spent the last 3 months in planning and final training as a group - in a Lashkar terrorist camp in the Kashmir province of Pakistan. It is reported that he terrorist in Indian custody spent 1.5 years in Pakistan training for the event.

The group Lashkar's new expanded stated goal is to help institute Islamic rule throughout India by using terrorist attacks on the country.

Secretary of State Rice has arrived in New Delhi to meet with Indian government officials.

Indian movie stars and sports figures join Mumbai citizens to protest last week's failure by the government to prevent the attack - and once it started to terminate the event in a timely manner – instead allowing the event to go on for 60 hours.

A US intelligence agency says - the group that perpetrated the event is the same group that bombed Mumbai passenger trains during rush hour in 2006, murdering 200.

Live NBC presentation by US lawmakers – states that Pakistan is the world's most major threat to nuclear proliferation to terrorist groups.

The news media is reporting that 5 terrorists got away – they will later say 10 got away.

According to one news report, four of the terrorists, two of them dead, had connections with Britain and may have been British muzlum citizens.

The Maharashtra Chief Minister Vilasrao Deshmukh told Associated Press that two British-born Pakistanis were among the eight gunmen arrested by Indian authorities.

Another news report, carried on the Indian NDTV news channel, suggested there may have been a total of 40 terrorists, 29 of them from Pakistan and the rest from Bangladesh.

A terrorist backpack was discovered by the Indian commandos contained 400 rounds of ammunition. It is understood that some of the gunmen were carrying bags of almonds to eat during a long siege – and that they were high on steroids, cocaine and LSD. The terrorists had foreign currency and credit cards.

Not only were they well armed with assault rifles and hand grenades, but they knew how to use them. An Indian commando spoke: "It's obvious they were trained somewhere ... not everyone can handle the AK series of weapons or throw grenades like that."

DOW 8320.00 before start
Pork Bellies are at 92.12
Yen starts around 93.21 drops to 92.89
Gold is at $777 at 6:30AM Central - drops $775 drops $767 this activity is occurring 2 hours prior to the start of the trading day
Oil is $47.01 a barrel.
Wholesale gas is at 1.05 a gallon wholesale – in Detroit retail is at $1.55 a gallon

Auto makers ask for $34B:
GM - $18B - will cut 32K jobs and cut "vehicle lines" down
Ford - $ 9B – make electric vehicles – closes MI Truck Plant
Chrysler - $7B

Toyota sales fall to lowest level in over 20 years. There is currently a backlog of over 5M new vehicles sitting in storage throughout the US – about a 6 month supply.

Citibank is paying the New York Mets $400M over the next 20 years for the use of the Citibank name on the Mets baseball stadium. (And of course Citibank has asked for many $B to bail them out of a bad financial position)

Nixon Whitehouse Tapes newly release from 1972 - show Nixon as being extremely ruthless, cynical and profane in conversations.

Obama plans a morning news conference. Every time he has held a news conference since he won the election - the DOW has ended in the positive for that session. Arizona Governor Richardson will be nominated for the Secretary of Commerce position within the Obama Cabinet.

PajamaGrams.com   for a pajama-gram

Delta to cut flight capacity citing 9% lower demand for air travel projected for 2009.

The Pope has publicly urged banks to help families experience financial problems.

USA- armless women flies solo in airplane.

Tennessee, 1 in 6 citizens are using food stamps.

49 states flunk college affordability says a government agency. (California used to give away free college education including free law school) The cost of college in the US is quickly getting out of reach of the middle class.

December 4, 2008 Thursday

December 4, 2008 Thursday

09:30 AM Central - the end of Day VIII - and the start of DAY IX – hour 192 - since the beginning of the event and 132 hours since the end of the event – 6.5 days after the "end" of the event.

Secretary of State Rice is still in New Delphi shaking hands and posing for pictures shaking hands.

The lone surviving terrorist has been identified as 21 year old Mohammad Kasab, a Pakistani national and a member of Lashkar-i Taiba.

Lashkar is a paramilitary wing of the Pakistani muzlum fundamentalist organization Markaz Dawa-Wal-Irshad.

Lashkar was founded in 1980, but up until 1993 operated mainly outside India. In the late 1990s Lashkar became the most influential Sunni paramilitary organization in the region.

In 2000 Lashkar carried out a series of terrorist attacks in India. Following 911 - September 11, 2001 - stories circulated that Lashkar had prior knowledge of the New York twin towers attack. Lashkar claimed responsibility for the Mumbai railway bombings of 2006 in which over 200 were murdered during rush hour.

Mumbai police sources say they have succeeded in reconstructing the terrorists movement – using the Garmin GPS device set that was seized after the event.

Chapter Eight

THE JEWISH COMMUNITY CENTER TIMELINE

THE JEWISH COMMUNITY CENTER TIMELINE

Wednesday night November 26, 2008

9:00 PM Mumbai time

Five – two man teams – land in Bombay Harbor and then split up. Four terrorists went to the Taj Mahal Hotel, two to the Jewish Community Center - The Chabad House/Nariman House, Kasab and another terrorist set off by taxi towards the railway station, and two terrorists headed for the Café Leopold restaurant – to begin their attacks at 09:20 PM.

11AM Central - One hour and 30 minutes into the event – The Jewish Community Center a.k.a. Nariman House a.k.a. Chabad House has been seized by the terrorists.

04:00 PM Central Wednesday – 04:00 AM Thursday India - Immediately after the first moments of the attack, India's elite National Security Guard was dispatched from New Delhi. They arrived in Mumbai at 4am – 7 hours after the start of the event. By 7:00 AM they will have command posts around Nariman House/The Chabad House. They are wearing black jumpsuits with balaclavas, are carrying large bow knives, Glock pistols and submachine guns.

09:05 PM Central Wednesday – 09:05 AM Thursday in India- The first reports come in that an Israeli Rabbi, his wife and two children are being held hostage at the Jewish Community Center – a.k.a. The Chabad House. But – they have been held captive since hour 1 of this event.

This is the Mumbai headquarters of an ultra-Orthodox Jewish outreach group. The house serves as an educational center, a synagogue and offers drug prevention services.

Other families also live at the house which is large, multi-storied (I think 5 stories) and appears to be constructed of cement and brick.

"It seems that the terrorists commandeered a police vehicle which allowed them easy access to the area of the Chabad house and they then threw a grenade at a gas pump nearby," said Rabbi Zalman Shmotkin, a spokesman for the Lubavitch movement in New York, adding the attackers then "stormed the Chabad house." (Kasab confessed to blowing up a gas pump)

Residents tried to protect the Jewish center, clashing with the gunmen and throwing rocks at them in an effort to drive the terrorists away, said Puran Doshi, a local businessman who lives nearby. The crowd eventually retreated under fire from the terrorists, who threw several grenades, wounding one man and murdering three others he said. "They fired indiscriminately into the crowd," Doshi said.

Sanjay Bhasme, 40, who lives in the building behind Chabad house, said he notified the police after the shooting began about 9:45 p.m., but no police arrived for more than 30 minutes — and only after he'd repeatedly telephoned for help.

November 27, 2008 Thanksgiving Thursday

12:01 AM Central Thursday – 12:01 PM Thursday in India –

At the Jewish Community Center, a woman, the family's cook, and a child – Moshe Holtzberg, aged two – escape.

After being shot at and hiding in a closet on the first floor for 12 hours - the nanny hears the child cry and leaves the closet on the first floor. She goes up to the second floor and finds the baby between the unconscious parents, picks up the baby and escapes the building as automatic gunfire rages inside the building.

Moshe's trousers are covered in blood and he has a handprint on his back where he was struck so hard he is rendered unconscious for about 12 hours. He is now an orphan. His mother and father, Rabbi Gavriel Holtzberg, are later found to have been tortured then murdered inside the house.

He is now an orphan. His mother and father, Rabbi Gavriel Holtzberg, are later found to have been tortured then murdered inside the house.

04:00 AM Central Thursday – 16:00 PM Thursday in India –

At the Jewish Community Center 30 more commandos joined police officers in the street – while the Elite special forces team is already on site watching from neighboring roof tops, (with press standing next to them chatting during this ongoing event)

06:00 AM Central Thursday – 18:00 PM Thursday in India –
At the Chabad House, a gunman calling himself "Imran" calls Indian media and says, in the Urdu dialect: "Ask the government to talk to us and we will release the hostages. Are you aware how many people have been killed in Kashmir? Are you aware how your army has killed Muslims? Are you aware how many of them have been killed in Kashmir this week?"

09:30 AM Central –
A Rabbi is currently being held hostage sat the Jewish Community Center.

11:30 AM Central Thursday – 23:30 PM Thursday in India – Eight more hostages are freed from Chabad House.

05:30 PM Central – hour 32 –
The terrorists are holding hostages at the Jewish Community Center and the Oberoi Hotel.

9:00 PM Central - hour 36.5 –
Security forces are now going door to door in the Oberoi hotel and have also entered the Jewish Community Center.

07:30 PM Central – Day II - hour 34 –
There are at least 3 Simultaneous hostage situations are ongoing in the city of Mumbai.

Security forces have landed on the roof of the Jewish Community Center via a helicopter and CNN has a live feed of this assault – I hope the terrorists aren't watching the assault on TV as I am at the moment. I could hear a live conversation by 3 commandoes outside the Jewish Center – which was captured and fed to the US-CNN.

An Indian commando team rappels from helicopters during the insertion into the Jewish Community Center and then a large explosion rocks the building and blows a gaping hole in the wall.

Unfortunately we will later discover that all 5 hostages have been tortured and murdered prior to or perhaps during this insertion.

The Chabad House name is getting co-mingled with the name Nariman House – we are given 2 Jewish Community Center names. Later it will be determined that the Nariman House is located next door to the Chabad house and that a terrorist was seen jumping from the roof of the Chabad House to the Nariman House – taking the fight from the Chabad House to the Nariman House.

It is not known at this time but the battle for the Jewish Community Center will go on for about 11.5 hours – after the helicopter lands the commandoes on the roof.

The Jewish Community Center is run by the ultra-orthodox Jewish outreach group Chabad Lubavitch.

Indian army snipers in buildings opposite the Jewish Community Center – Chabad/Nariman House open fire. Then commandos rope down from a hovering helicopter on to the roof of the Jewish Community Center enter.

Associated Press: This insertion "was punctuated by gunshots and explosions - and at one point an intense exchange of fire that lasted several minutes - as forces cleared it floor by floor".

By Friday afternoon, the security forces had control of the top two floors.

Just after dusk, a massive explosion shook the Jewish Community Center, blowing out windows in neighboring buildings. Gunfire and smaller explosions followed the first blast.

One camouflaged commando came out with a bandage on his forehead, while soldiers fired smoke grenades into the building and a steady stream of gunfire reverberated across narrow alleys.

November 28, 2008 Friday

12:30 AM Central – Day II - hour 38

03:00 AM Central Friday – 15:00 PM Friday in India -
Indian police claim to have control of the Oberoi. They have so
far recovered 24 bodies.

At Chabad House, commandos soon report they have taken the
top two floors in what is dubbed Operation Black Tornado.

The death toll reaches 143, with 288 injured.

04:30 AM Central – 16:30 PM Friday Mumbai
The commandos enter a fifth-floor apartment from the roof and
drape a red flag in the window—this is a signal to others on
their team. It becomes clear they don't have radios. In order to
communicate with each other they either speak to each other in
person or use their cell phones.

05:00 AM Central Friday – 17:00 PM Mumbai Friday
The sniper teams continued shooting into the fourth floor of the
Jewish Community Center - through broken glass and curtains.

The security forces fire a succession of rockets into the fourth
floor, taking out what little remained of the wall to obscure the
view into the building. The building's upper walls are now
thoroughly pockmarked with bullet holes and soot-covered
from explosions.

Commandos can be seen walking around the first floor, and
moving around the stairwell. They lean over the roof and shoot
down into the windows. More explosions and small arms fire
can be heard.

05:30 AM Central Friday – 17:30 PM Mumbai Friday
The fourth floor of Chabad/Nariman House explodes shaking all of south Bombay and sending everyone nearby to the ground looking for cover.

Another massive explosion is reported from The Chabad House, when commandos blow up an outer wall to gain access to the compound.

Commandos enter the building, emptying machine gun clips in quick succession.

06:00 AM Central Friday – 18:00 PM Friday in India - Chabad House is still under terrorist control. Commandoes are still on the roof of the Chabad House (a.k.a. the Chabad Center) – 10.5 hours after they were inserted by a helicopter.

The End at the Jewish Community Center

07:00 AM Central Friday – 19:00 PM Friday in India -

Day II - Hour 44.5

At The Chabad House/Nariman House, Indian Security Forces leave, firing their weapons in the air, to signal that at last The Jewish Community Center has been liberated. The bodies of six hostages and two gunmen are found inside. The termination of this situation took 11.5 hours from insertion by helicopter to completion - but came 46.5 hours after the start of the occupation.

Rabbi Gavriel Holtzberg, 29, will be found by his colleague, Rabbi Goldberg, lying slumped on the ground of his living quarters wrapped in tefillin, a prayer aid containing the Hebrew scrolls. On his bedside table is found copies of Jewish holy texts along with a book entitled: "How to protect yourself when terrorists come to your house."

08:30 AM Central – hour 47 –
Crowds are growing in the streets across from known terrorist sites.

Crowds are growing in the streets across from the Jewish Community Center also – literally packing the streets – taking control of the streets – so that a vehicle cannot drive through – and the crowds are angry.

It appears that the media is co-mingling the term Chabad House and Nariman House as the Jewish Community Center – as CNN has just announced that 5 hostages and 2 terrorists are dead at the Chabad house – which was the death toll CNN had attached to the Nariman House minutes ago. Later we will find out a terrorist jumped from the Chabad House to the Nariman House and took the fight with him.

Israeli Foreign Minister speaks at press conference – same information again – 5 hostages murdered and 2 terrorists dead at the Jewish Community Center.

06:00 PM Central - Day III – hour 56.5 –
There appears to be plenty of ammunition for the terrorists- as gunfire is still being heard in front of the Taj Mahal.

Finally as I was about to change the channel – away from CNN - 10 seconds perhaps only 5 seconds of live video footage outside the Jewish Community Center is shown – the streets are packed with people chanting and screaming – almost a riot – we would call this a riot in Detroit - the citizens of Mumbai are very mad and screaming in the streets at the moment.

The citizens of Mumbai have so filled the streets in front of the Jewish Community Center– you could not drive a car or any vehicle - through this screaming – chanting - antagonized crowd/mob. (Maybe this is why CNN is not showing any live video footage – Mumbai citizens are rioting in the streets calling for an end to this event)

Chapter Nine

TAJ MAHAL HOTEL TIMELINE

TAJ MAHAL HOTEL TIMELINE

09:30 PM – Nov 26 – Zero Hour – Wednesday Evening

10:30 PM – hour 1
Terrorists are inside the Oberoi and Taj Mahal hotels firing automatic weapons and murdering innocents.

11:30 PM – Nov 26 – hour 2
The lobbies of both the Oberoi and Taj Mahal hotels are on fire.

Police now surround the Taj, but no one knows what's going on inside. What is going on inside is wholesale murder as the terrorists walk through the hotel firing automatic weapons and throwing hand grenades at anything that moved.

12:30 AM – Nov 27 – hour 3 - Thursday
A British guest escapes from the Taj Mahal and tells Indian television that gunmen are taking hostages and looking for people carrying British and American passports to execute.

The exact time the security forces start entering the Taj Mahal is not clear but it is believed some Indian security forces start to enter the hotel about 3 to 5 hours after the event begins.

When the security forces first enter the hotel they are led around by hotel employees. The only idea they have about what lies ahead is that the "bad guys" have automatic weapons and explosives.

From an interview with an Indian security force commando, "Then we heard gunshots on the second floor and we rushed toward the fired shots," he said. "While taking cover we found that there were 30 to 50 bodies lying dead. At that point we also came under fire. The moment they saw us, they hurled grenades toward us."

The Taj Mahal's enormous atrium and large dome make the sounds of gunfire and explosions endlessly reverberate. It is impossible for the security forces to pinpoint what direction the gunfire is originating from.

01:00 AM – Nov 27 – hour 3.5
Guests and staff are still trying to escape from the two hotels.

A German media executive dies in a fall from the front of the Taj Mahal trying to climb out a window to get out of the building.

From outside the hotel, people can be seen silhouetted against windows. Some raise their fists vainly against the glass; others flick their lights on and off in distress. A couple take turns waving a white flag.

01:30 AM – Nov 27 – hour 4
"Four or five" terrorists have now taken an unknown number of guests hostage in the two hotels.

At the Taj Mahal there are 50 Korean hostages. Shortly afterwards, there is an explosion at the Taj Mahal.

02:30 AM – Nov 27 – hour 5 –
20 people hiding in a library area escape with the aid of security forces with a terrorist hiding among them. Businessman Hugh Brown, later says, "When he got out with us, he started shooting some of the people as they were leaving the room. He was then dealt with by the security forces. He pretended to be one of us in the room. He had a rucksack which he wouldn't allow us to look into. He said it was private property. In retrospect, we probably should have done something."

03:30 AM – Nov 27 – hour 6
Naval commandos storm hotel

04:30 AM - Nov 27 – hour 7
Terrorists are throwing grenades from the roof of the Taj Mahal to stop police from entering the hotel.

Hundreds of guests have now been evacuated from the Taj Mahal Hotel, but others, are still held hostage inside. Others – trapped and hiding in their hotel rooms but not captured – cry for help from windows. Firefighters on large ladder trucks are breaking windows to reach them – risking their lives as the event is far from over.

More than 200 people evacuated

05:45 AM – Nov 27
26 of the 50 Koreans who had been trapped in the Taj Mahal are reported to have escaped unharmed. They hid together for five hours in a conference room. No news of what happen to the other 24 Koreans ever reported.

06:15AM – Nov 27
In the Taj Mahal, on the 15th floor, security forces are escorting hotel guests out of the hotel. But the hotel is not under control at this point – firefights between security forces and terrorists will go on at this location for another 24 hours.

06:30 AM – Nov 27 – hour 9
Army takes over area, NSG enters hotel

07:00 AM - Nov 27 - hour 9.5

As the sun comes up, the Taj Mahal is surrounded by armed police, ambulances, and fire engines. Periodic firing is heard, and flames and smoke still escape from the roof.

09:30AM – Nov 27 – Thursday - hour 12
A terrorist calling himself Sahadullah calls Indian television and says: "There are seven of us inside the Oberoi. We want all Mujahideens held in India released and only after that will we release the people. Release all the Mujahideens, and Muslims living in India should not be troubled."

Anti Terrorism Squad member Roy said four more gunmen were killed at the Taj Mahal.

The terrorists are currently holding hostages in some of the hotels.

The Taj Mahal Hotel caught fire and is burning out of control at this moment.

10:30 AM – Nov 27 – hour 13
Gun battle reported from inside the Taj Mahal

12:00 PM – Nov 27 – hour 14.5
Noon 50 evacuated

02:00 PM – Nov 27 – hour 16.5
State Police Chief Roy says the Taj Mahal hostages have all been released. This is not the case – this is the first false "all clear".

03:00 PM – Nov 27 – hour 17.5
Six bodies recovered - Ten grenade explosions over the next hour

04:00 PM – Nov 27 – hour 18.5
About a dozen hostages leave the Taj Mahal and climb into ambulances. Three bodies, covered in white sheets, are wheeled out of the hotel.

04:30 PM – Nov 27 – hour 19
Terrorists set fire to a room on the 4th floor

05:00 PM – Nov 27 – hour 19.5
Gunfire and explosions are heard at the Taj Mahal as security teams launch an assault on the terrorists.

07:00 PM – Nov 27 – hour 21.5
New weapons' firing is currently going off within the Taj Mahal Hotel, Oberoi Hotel and the Jewish Community Center

07:30 PM – Nov 27 – hour 22
More NSG commandos arrive, enter hotel

09:00 PM – Nov 27 – hour 23.5
Another explosion just occurred at the Taj Mahal Hotel - rated by Forbes magazine as one of the most luxurious hotels in the world.

Supposedly the Taj Mahal Hotel has been "cleared" of terrorists (again for the second time – this is not the case)

11:00 PM – Nov 27 – hour 26.5
Operations continue

11:30 PM – Nov 27 - hour 26
State officials say the siege at the Taj Mahal has ended, and the last three terrorists have been killed. Unfortunately this is the third time this will be announced.

Dipak Dutta, rescued from the Taj Mahal, tells how troops escorting him through the corridors told him not to look down at any of the bodies. "A lot of chef trainees were massacred in the kitchen," he adds.

Two loud explosions and gunfire are heard at the Taj Mahal. Electricity is cut off from the floors where it is believed gunmen still roam.

12:30 AM – Nov 28 - Friday – hour 27
No new news on the Taj Mahal operations for the next 13 hours.

It has been reported by the Indian Government News Agency that the terrorists had set up "Control Room Head Quarters" in rooms in both the Taj Mahal and the Oberio – "months in advance".

12:30 PM – Nov 28 – hour 39
No news on the situation at the Taj Mahal for 12 hours

3:00 PM - Nov 28 – hour 41.5
PM Marine commandos recover explosives in Taj.

4.00 PM - Nov 28 – 42.5
Dead bodies recovered from the Taj by Naval Commandos.

06:00 PM - Nov 28 – 44.5
There is more shooting at the Taj Mahal as Indian forces begin firing grenades at the Taj, where at least one gunman is holed up in the ballroom – we will later find out with 200 hostages.

7:30 PM - Nov 28 – hour 46
There are fresh explosions and gun shots at Taj Hotel.

8:30 PM - Nov 28 – Friday - hour 47
Reported that one terrorist left at the Taj.

01:00AM – Nov 28 – Saturday – hour 52.5
A commando officer reports that they have found 15 bodies in a room at the Taj Mahal Hotel.

93 hostages are released/freed from the Oberio Hotel while a large explosion in the street outside of the Taj Mahal occurs during a live CNN interview.

02:30 AM - Nov 29 - Saturday in India – hour 53
Fires are raging on first floor. Black smoke is appearing to come from the second floor – gunfire is heard frequently — there is an ongoing apparent gun battle.

03:30 AM - Nov 29 – Saturday in India – hour 54
Indian commandos state that the Taj Hotel is now under control. However they are still conducting room to room searches. <u>This is the forth time the government has announced the building is clear – it will not be cleared for another 6 hours.</u>

Then 10 minutes after the "all clear" announcement by security forces – as if the terrorists were watching live TV -

03:40 AM - 04:10 AM - Nov 29
There are reports of five explosions at the Taj.

05:00 AM - Nov 29 – hour 56.5
A new revised estimate of 2-3 terrorists in the Taj is released by the government. Nothing happens for the next 2.5 hours.

The Final Assault Is About To Begin

07:30 AM - Nov 29 - Saturday in India - Hour 58 - of DAY III

Gunfire is still erupting out of the Taj Mahal Hotel – it appears there is no end of this event in sight – no new video feeds from CNN.

Smoke is billowing from the ground floor of the Taj Mahal.

What is to be the final assault and final battle of this terrorist event begins as Indian Security Forces and terrorists are fighting each other from room to room inside the Taj Mahal.

Three terrorists are killed and the body of one terrorist is thrown out a window onto the street - to the cheers of those on the streets.

Sniffer dogs are led into the hotel to search for bombs and bodies.

08:00 AM - Nov 29 – hour 58.5
The Taj Mahal is still exploding, burning and smoking.

09:00 AM -Nov 29 - Saturday in India – hour 59.5
During the final assault by commandoes on the Taj Mahal – the security teams find rooms full of bodies at the Taj Mahal – as the official death toll climbs past 195.

The building has experienced multiple hand grenade explosions and fires throughout the entire structure and many rooms are gutted. The outside of the structure shows signs of fire. It will take a lot of work to put this hotel back the state it was in prior to the attack.

09:30AM – November 29, 2008

Saturday in India

Hour 60 - The End

The FINAL battle of this event will be at the Taj Mahal.

This final battle of this terrorist event comes to an end with a final firefight in a Taj Mahal ballroom holding 200 hostages.

No information is released on the fate of the 200 hostages in the ballroom until a week later when it is announced all 200 hostages were freed.

The government security forces announce a 5th "all clear" at the Taj Mahal.

CNN announces the end came to the Mumbai Massacre at hour 60.

Chapter Ten

OBEROI HOTEL TIME LINE

OBEROI HOTEL TIME LINE

09:30 PM - Nov 26 - Wednesday – Zero Hour

09:00 PM – Nov 26 - Muzlum terrorists land on the city/island of Mumbai (formally called Bombay) at Bombay Harbor in 2-3 or perhaps 4 boats and attack 10 sites simultaneously (all within an hour or so), using automatic weapons and hand grenades.

The shooting starts at about 9:30 p.m. local Mumbai time.

10:30 PM – Mumbai Time - Nov 26 - hour 1
Terrorists are inside the Oberoi and Taj Mahal hotels firing automatic weapons at innocents.

11:30 PM - Nov 26 – hour 2
The lobbies of both the Oberoi and Taj Mahal hotels are on fire.

Police say seven sites are under attack. The death toll rises to four – but really is already well over the 100 mark.

07:00 AM - Nov 27 - Thursday in India – hour 9.5
7.5 hours pass with no new developments – as now the friends of those trapped inside start to gather in the streets

07:00 PM Central Wednesday – 07:00 AM Thursday in India-
As the sun comes up - at the Oberoi Hotel, friends of those trapped inside start to gather in the streets.

11:30 AM - Nov 27 - hour 14
Confused reports come in from the government.

A state official says "police and commandos have begun operations against the terrorists at the Oberoi but there could still be 100-200 guests and staff trapped there.

09:00 PM - Nov 27 - Thursday - hour 23.5
Huge flames shoot from an upper floor of the Oberoi.

Commandos are reportedly fighting room-to-room battles with terrorists inside the Oberoi.

Half an hour later, 45 hostages are reported freed from the Oberoi, but 35 remain inside.

The Oberio Hotel is currently on fire.

November 27, 2008 Thanksgiving Thursday

12:01 AM Central Thursday – 12:01 PM Thursday in India –

08:00 AM Central Thursday – 20:00 PM Thursday in India –
Huge flames shoot from an upper floor of the Oberoi.

Commandos are reportedly fighting room-to-room battles with terrorists.

Half an hour later, 45 hostages are reported freed from the Oberoi, but 35 remain inside.

05:30 AM Mumbai – Nov 28 – Friday – Day II - hour 32

8.5 hours go by with no change in the situation at the Oberoi.

Explosions are still rocking the streets of Mumbai.

The terrorists are holding hostages at the Jewish Community Center and the Taj Mahal and the Oberoi Hotels.

07:00 AM Mumbai - 07:00 PM Central – Day II – hour 33.5 – New gunfire is currently going off within the Taj Mahal Hotel, Oberoi Hotel and the Jewish Community Center.

09:00 AM – Nov 28 - Friday - hour 36.5
Security forces are now going door to door in the Oberoi hotel and have also entered the Jewish Community Center.

10:00 AM – Nov 28 - hour 36.5
More guests, including a chef, a baby and people carrying luggage bearing Canadian flags, are led from the Oberoi.

11:30 AM – Nov 28 - hour 38
A police officer outside the Oberoi shouts through loudhailer that 93 guests have so far been rescued from the hotel. Almost simultaneously an explosion goes off inside the hotel.

At the Oberoi, dozens are still being held hostage.

An official says security forces have cleared the ground to the fourth floors, and the eighth to the 21st floors.

11:40 AM Nov 28 – hour 38 - Friday in India -Confused reports come in from the government.

A state official says "police and commandos have begun operations against the terrorists at the Oberoi but there could still be 100-200 guests and staff trapped there.

November 28 12:30 PM – Friday - hour 39

The End at the Oberio

93 hostages are released/freed from the Oberio Hotel (while a large explosion in the street outside of the Taj Mahal occurs during a live CNN interview)

Two dozen more people are rescued from the Oberoi Hotel. Those rescued are mainly air crews with Lufthansa and Air France.

It has been reported by the Indian Government News Agency that the terrorists had set up "Control Room Head Quarters" in rooms in both the Taj Mahal and the Oberio – "months in advance".

Indian security forces have killed the two last terrorists inside the Oberoi Hotel.

"The Oberoi Hotel is under our control," J.K. Dutt, director general of India's elite National Security Guard commando unit, told reporters, adding that 24 bodies had been found.

A 51-year-old from London - describing the scene when he was eventually led to safety - he said it was "carnage" with "blood and guts everywhere". For almost two days, a 51-year-old from London had locked himself in his room to escape the terrorists who were holding hostages several floors below. He spent his time listening to gunshots and explosions and communicating with the outside world on his phone and Blackberry. This was after the terrorists went ballistic - killing wildly in the initial raid on the Oberoi Wednesday night. It was very, very upsetting,' he told the BBC. "Just before I went to my room I had had dinner in the Kandahar restaurant. I have now found out that it was one of the restaurants where the terrorist attacks started. Unfortunately, the waitress who served me was one of the first to get murdered." Speaking of his relief, he added: "It is great to be out. It has been 48 hours, but without food and water - surrounded by explosions and gunshots and people running down corridors screaming.... it has been grim, very grim."

It has been reported by the Indian Government News Agency that the terrorists had set up "Control Room Headquarters" in hotel rooms in both the Taj Mahal and the Oberio – "weeks if not months in advance".

Chapter Eleven

Past major terrorist attacks on India

In India during past 7 months from July 2008 to November 2008 there were 70 terrorist bombing attacks which murdered 400.

Since 2004, nearly 4,000 people have been killed in India by terrorist violence.

India is a major victim of terror ranking second only to Iraq in terms of casualties.

December 1, 2008:
Almost immediately after the end of the Mumbai Massacre – a train is bombed in north east India – 30 are murdered.

Nov. 26, 2008:
The Mumbai Massacre – a series of shooting and grenade attacks, including two attacks on luxury hotels, kills at least 200 people and wound 300 in Mumbai - India's main commercial city – and rages on for 60 hours over a 3 day period.

Sept. 13, 2008:
At least five explosions in crowded shopping areas kill 21 and wound 100 in New Delhi, national capital.

July 26, 2008:
Some 16 small bombs explode in Ahmedabad, killing 45.

July 25, 2008:
Seven small bombs kill two in Bangalore, hub of India's technology industry.

May 13, 2008:
Seven bombs hit crowded markets and streets outside Hindu temples in Jaipur, killing 80.

Nov. 24, 2007:
Nearly simultaneous explosions rip courthouse complexes in Lucknow, Varanasi and Faizabad, killing 16.

Aug. 25, 2007:
Forty-three people killed by three explosions at park and street-side food stall in Hyderabad.

May 18, 2007:
Bomb during Friday prayers at historic mosque in Hyderabad kills 11 worshippers. Police later fatally shoot five people during clashes with Muslims protesting attack.

Feb. 19, 2007:
Train heading from India to Pakistan torn apart by two bombs, sparking fire that kills 68.

July 11, 2006:
Seven blasts rip through rail stations and commuter trains during rush hour in Mumbai, killing 200

March 7, 2006:
Three explosions rock Hindu temple and train station in Hindu holy city of Varanasi, killing 20.

Oct. 29, 2005:
Sixty-two people killed by three blasts at markets in New Delhi ahead of Hindu holiday of Wali.

Chapter Twelve

AFTER THE EVENT – THE ANALYSIS

And

Additional Information Discovered

Now the analysis of what has occurred in Mumbai begins.

Four months ago the president of the Fishermen's Union, Damodar Tandel, received a warning from another fisherman friend in the coastal state of Gujarat – that of the nearly 1,000 fishing boats that shuttle between Gujarat and Mumbai, some might be smuggling munitions and plastic explosives into Mumbai. Tandel relayed the message in a letter to the police chief in charge of Mumbai's port. The chief was asked about that letter last week, during the terrorist siege and said - "It was just a general statement - there was no specific information."

A group of terrorists seized hostages at a hospital in Mumbai. The Mumbai's anti-terrorism chief and two other top police officials arrived at the scene with policemen who were armed with antique .303 rifles. The three police leaders must not have realized the danger of the situation and were quickly murdered by automatic weapon gunfire.

Nariman House – The Jewish Community Center was ripped apart by an enormous explosion that killed everyone inside. The explosion was set off by the Indian Commandoes.

17 Policeman killed is the final total, as released by the Indian government after the event.

The number one motive for the attack seams to be to start a nuclear war between India and Pakistan.

Another motive is to just destabilize the 2 countries so internal terrorists groups can gain power.

Another new motive is that - internal Indian security forces were involved with Mumbai organized crime and this attack was staged as an event to cover up the murder of police, the

Anti Terrorism Squad Chief (ATS) and the Mumbai chief of police – who were hot on the trail of the organized crime figures.

Mumbai may have more Billionaires than any other city on earth. Mumbai apartments and home prices are among the highest in the world. Mumbai is getting richer and richer by the day as the business of making serious money drives Mumbai.

There is now an alternate theory of a local Hindu terrorist group lending assistance to the Lashkar group – with help from internal Indian security forces and muzlumz from the UK all funded by organized criminals in Mumbai.

Local Hindu terrorist groups have been engaged in subversive activities in the recent past - waging full-fledged freedom movements in several provinces. Despite using their large military force - India has failed to control these Hindu terrorists.

Mr. Sarkare of Mumbai's Anti-Terrorism Squad (ATS) said that they have arrested some people whose boat/taxi was used during the Mumbai terrorist attack - by the terrorists – calling them local operatives.

ATS has found that the water taxi used during the attack belonged to Sadhvi Ojha Thakur.

Mr. Sarkare says that Sadhvi Ojha decided to carry the terrorists to take revenge for the death of her boyfriend - though at this point the story is not clear as to when or where the water taxi was used.

A lesser known Indian terrorist group, Vibhinna Bharat, is being looked at as having been involved in the terrorist attack.

ATS has also taken custody of Mr. Surohit and Mr. Sadanand Pande, who they believe may have masterminded the plan as local operatives and sent them for "Narco Analysis".

Mr. Sarkare and Mr. Roy of ATS have said that they are investigating the possible links of Sadhvi and Surohit with the parliament attack case and the Assam blasts.

An Indian Congress spokesperson Mr. Ahmed today said that Hindu terrorism has taken life of 200 people in Mumbai.

A high ranking Indian government official has stated that there were local operatives from Mumbai who have been working with terrorists since 2007.

Then there is this story of trade routes and water rights – just a story but places a new twist on India and Pakistani relations.

Pakistan has opened three more routes for Pakistan -India trade. Pakistan has accepted all of India's demands during trade negotiations. One of Pakistan's demands regarding the trade route talks was refused. India refuses to release the water of the Chenab River and refuses to acknowledge the "Kashmiris" as a party to the Kashmir dispute. Some Pakistanis demanded that Pakistan should discontinue trade with India unless India conceded to releasing the Chenab River water and also solving the Kashmir issue.

Construction of dams on the Jhelum and Chenab rivers by India is blocking water from getting to Pakistan – and has destroyed 15 million acres of standing crops in the country. If the water diversion situation continues the entire Pakistani Punjab region could turn into desert and would become totally dependent on India for basic vegetables and grain. India may be violating the Indus Water Treaty. Fixing the human rights situation in

Kashmir and the water for Punjab issues appear to be in the very center of stabilizing Indian and Pakistani relations.

India has a history of problems between Hindus and Muslims and also between Hindus and Hindus. In 2002, the main opposition party, the BJP, was accused of being the biggest anti-Muslim entity in modern Indian history.

In 1948, Mahatma Gandhi, serving Indian Prime Minister was assassinated by members of his own religion who mimicked the beliefs of the BJP. Those that assassinated Mahatma Gandhi were intolerant of any religion except Hinduism.

In 1984, Indira, Gandhi the serving Prime Mister at the time, was shot 38 times while being assassinated by her 2 Sikh bodyguards, one who had been with her for 10 years. Indira had ordered the Indian army to attack the Sikh's holiest shrine, The Golden Temple in Amritsar. The assassins attempted an escape while in custody. One assassin was killed immediately the other was critically wounded and told his doctors that he was a member of a conspiracy that included a high-ranking army officer.

In 1991, in the town of Sriperempudur, Rajiv Gandhi the Prime Mister of India was assassinated by a woman who denoted explosives strapped to herself - presumably over the Indian military occupation of Sri Lanka, (an island nation at the very southern tip of India). Sri Lanka underwent a two decade long civil war which claimed 60K Sri Lankan lives. 26 were sentenced to death in the subsequent murder trial.

Footnote – some following ideas and concepts are from Time and Newsweek – and they are so solid I have recapitulated some of them and added a few more ideas here for you.

Chapter Thirteen

Who is Involved?

Who may be involved?

Each one of these players provides its own unique function to the muzlum war machine. I believe they are all acting with each other – all the time – they are one.

Markaz Dawa-Wal-Irshad – is a Pakistani Muslim fundamentalist organization of which - Lashkar is the paramilitary wing. Markaz is the head of the beast. All of the following organizations listed here below are a different arm and leg making up a "body of terror" with Markaz as the "head of the beast".

Lashkar-e-Toiba (Army of the Pure) – Lashkar was founded in 1980, but up until 1993 operated mainly outside India. The group became influential in Afghanistan in 1990. In the late 1990s Lashkar became the most influential Sunni paramilitary organization in the region. Currently they are based near Lahore in Pakistan. (This is where the Mumbai terrorists embarked from) Lashkar's goal is to remove India from Kashmir. Their expanded goal is also to restore Islamic rule throughout India. This group provides the cannon fodder.

Indian intelligence sources say this group has backers within Pakistan's ISI. It also has historic links to both the Taliban and al-Qaeda.

India's National Security Adviser Narayanan said in 2006 that Lashkar is part of the "al-Qaeda compact" and is "as large and as omnipotent" as Osama bin Laden's group.

(I say Lashkar is just an extension - a franchise belonging to the same company – if you will – and unfortunately everyone wants to focus in on Lashkar when the head of the beast is

Markaz Dawa-Wal-Irshad and additional personnel come from Jamaat-ud-Dawa, the common theme here is Kashmir)

Jamaat-ud-Dawa – was formed by Hafiz Mohammad Saeed in 2002 after the Lashkar group was outlawed. This group runs medical clinics, schools and housing projects, especially in Pakistani Kashmir and maintains a charitable and public face for the Lashkar. Their main madrassa is located in the town of Muzaffarabad. This group has a main political complex at Muridke, (just west of Lahore, Pakistan's second largest city, near the Indian border). This 150-acre complex, called Markaz-e-Taybah, or Center of the Pious, has a school of 3,000 economically distressed students, a farm, a hospital and a mosque.

Students Islamic Movement of India (SIMI) – was formed in 1977. This group is not as interested in Kashmir as Lashkar or Jaish-e-Mohammed. This group may have close connections to Chicago's Muslim community. Some Indian security officials believe that the "SIMI" group is just the "Indian Mujahideen" organization renamed.

Jaish-e-Mohammed – was formed in 2000 under the leadership of Maulana Masood Azhar. Azhar was in an Indian jail for Kashmir related terrorist activity and was released in exchange for Indian passengers on an Indian Airlines jet which had been hijacked to Afghanistan. This group is responsible for an attack on India's parliament in December 2001 that brought India and Pakistan to the brink of war.

Jaish-e-Mohammed is believed to also have close links to al-Qaeda and bin Laden through a religious school in Karachi.

Harkat-ul-Jehadi Islami - was formed in 1992 in Dhaka, Bangladesh. This group has joined forces with the groups mentioned above at various times. This terrorist group is believed to be behind twin blasts in Hyderabad in 2007. This group has become stronger since the massacre of Muslims by hard-line Hindu nationalists in Gujarat in 2002.

Jammu Kashmir Liberation Front – is the leading terrorist group from Kashmir. This group was started by Yasin Malik. This group is made up of Afghan immigrants. This group is comprised of Islamic Afghan Mujahideen fighters who needed a war to fight after the Soviet-Afghan conflict ended and walked over to Kashmir to engage in their profession, the killing of other human beings as sanctioned legal by Islamic religious leaders. I believe that this group was also represented at Mumbai.

Sahni, the director of the New Delhi based Institute for Conflict Management, says there is no real evidence "of any operational linkages between al-Qaeda and these groups – which I personally disagree with. I believe all of these groups are very related to one another, they are one. And we now know there is an absolute linkage with the Taliban.

These seven separate groups are not separate and provide the necessary but different specific functions which are necessary to fielding and training an army of mass murderers. These groups work with each other in sophisticated ways. There have been instances in the past of the groups establishing joint operations.

To avoid police infiltration and compromising of the planned event - while planning an event the size of the Mumbai attacks it is believed that the terrorists have decentralized into small 3 to 10 man cells as verified by Kasab the captured terrorist. It is believed that each group or team of terrorists attacking a specific target in Mumbai was unlikely to have known or been aware of all the participants, all of the targets nor the entire plan. Kasab, the captured terrorist, unknowingly verifies this concept. There were 2 other terrorists at the train station besides Kasab and his partner, that Kasab did not know, who were also murdering innocents at the train station.

Sahni the director of the New Delhi based Institute for Conflict Management has said that previous experience suggests that an operation of the complexity of the Mumbai attacks would be directed by handlers based outside India. They would design a plan and then contact terrorists within their networks based in India to carry out various missions – such as renting a safe house, delivering explosives to a safe house, the buying equipment – preparing for the event. Again this is verified by the captured terrorist Kasab.

None of the India-based operatives would know one another or even meet. Contact with the handler would always be through a public phone to make it difficult to trace calls. If a terrorist operative were picked up by police, there would be no way for him to identify fellow terrorists.

"It assures total anonymity," Sahni told TIME last year. "The handler is in Kashmir, Bangladesh or Pakistan, and the people here don't know each other. It's the most significant tactical shift in the near past and is a model for international terrorism in the future."

The Chief Minister of Mumbai, reportedly said - Two British-born Pakistanis were among eight gunmen seized by Indian commandos - who stormed buildings to free hostages.

As many as seven of the terrorists may have British connections and some could be from Leeds and Bradford where "London's July 7" bombers lived, a source said. Two Britons were among eight terrorists being held, according to Mumbai's chief minister Vilasrao Deshmukh. At least nine others are reportedly dead. The eight arrested were captured by commandos after they stormed two hotels and a Jewish centre to free hostages today. One security official said: "There is growing concern about British involvement in the attacks."

Another short statement by the government - Three terrorists arrested at the Taj Mahal have been officially identified as a Pakistani national and two Indians. Another is reported to be a Mauritian national.

It is known that dozens of British-born Pakistanis have traveled to Pakistan to train in its terrorist camps in recent years. A security source said recently: "Pakistan's terrorist camps are full and many of the people inside these camps are British".

There is speculation that a British Al Qaeda suspect reportedly killed by a U.S. missile strike in Pakistan in mid-November 2008 - may have helped plot the Mumbai attack. Rashid Rauf was among five killed in a missile attack in a tribal area in North Waziristan, Pakistan.

Indian officials are convinced that the attack on Mumbai was organized by Lashkar. They also believe that Lashkar does not act without the sanction of some part of the Pakistan government – although how far up the political chain of command is unknown. This tells us that the Mumbai Massacre event was most likely sparked by the 600 year old Kashmir property dispute conflict

The hijacked Indian fishing boat used by the terrorists had equipment for 15 men on board when it was discovered adrift – suggesting that several gunmen could still be at large as fifteen winter jackets were found and fifteen toothbrushes among other items.

Indian security officials say one of two Indians arrested for illegally buying mobile phone SIM cards used by the gunmen in the Mumbai attacks- is an Indian counter-terrorism agent who may have been on an undercover mission.

The other man arrested, Tauseef Rahman, allegedly bought the SIM cards by providing fake documents, including identification cards from dead people - a police spokesman said. This Bangladeshi national bought cell phone SIM (subscriber identity modules) cards for the attackers at several locations inside India,

Officials have said that an Indian citizen who was arrested in February in northern India – was carrying hand-drawn sketches of hotels, the train terminal and other sites that were later attacked – and is being brought to Mumbai for further questioning.

12-10-08 USA cable news source – 10 terrorists may have gotten away.

Indian Coast Guard officials said they found an Indian fishing trawler – which was probably used to drop the terrorists off - after finding the abandoned fishing boat drifting near the shore. The fishing boat's captain's dead body was found inside the vessel, along with communications equipment.

Indian security forces have recovered credit cards and the militant's ID cards as well as a vast arsenal of grenades, AK-47 magazines, shells and knives.

It is thought the terrorists gained entrance to the Taj Mahal and Oberoi hotels by pretending to be staff and hotel guests as well as having rented rooms in both the Taj Mahal and the Oberoi.

Witnesses reported that the terrorist attackers in Mumbai were like a "jihadist infantry". There were up to 100 young men in their twenties when they split up and were striding in groups to their target locations, lobbing grenades and using AK-47 assault rifles to murder terrified bystanders.

About an hour before the shooting started, villagers on the shore in South Mumbai – on Bombay Harbor - saw a group of 10 young men – who were strangers to them - climbing out of an inflatable raft. They reported this incident o local police, who did nothing.

A short note on a possible explanation of – "where did the terrorists guns and ammo" – the munitions - come from - and who brought them into Mumbai?

After the Mumbai attack it was announced by Pakistan - that after the Pakistan army assault on the Red Mosque in July 2007 a large cache of weapons was seized. The army and police seized ammunition, machine guns, assault rifles, pistols, rockets, rocket launchers, and hand grenades. The arms disappeared from the police station in Aapbara, Pakistan where the equipment was stored. 10 police officials, including the head of the Aapbara police station where the weapons disappeared from - have been arrested. The Red Mosque in the past has frequently been used as a staging point for "terrorists" or "freedom fighters" on their way to fight India in Kashmir.

In case you missed this from the beginning of the book – from the "Forward"

India's most notorious international organized crime boss is Dawood Ibrahim. He has ties to al-Qaida and many terrorist groups though his international crime ring which has been called the **"D-Gang"** by the Indian press. He stands accused of orchestrating the 1993 terrorist bombings in Mumbai, which killed over 250 innocents. The munitions used in the 1993 terrorist attack were smuggled into Mumbai after they were brought in by boat from the coast - from Pakistan - by Dawood

Ibrahim's men. The modus operandi of the munitions entry into 1993 Mumbai is almost **an exact copy of what just has happened in this 2008 Mumbai Massacre**. There have been numerous criminal convictions in the 1993 Mumbai terrorist bombing case. Ibrahim was charged, but never brought to trial, because police could never apprehend him.

Chapter Fourteen

The Captured Terrorist – Kasab

The Captured Terrorist – Kasab:

Regarding the captured terrorist - there are reports that the terrorist speaks fluent English, suggesting that he is from Pakistan's relatively wealthy middle classes – making him a "high quality" militant - well educated.

The 21-year-old terrorist in captivity, who is a Pakistani national from the Punjab region, said that his father, Amir, introduced him to a commander of Lashkar-e-Taiba. The commander, known as "chacha" (uncle), paid the father. Security experts say that payment is one of three main recruitment tools used by Islamist extremists. The other two are acceptance into the madrassas, or Islamic seminaries scattered across Pakistan, and threats of violence often directed at the families of those being recruited.

Experts believe it is unlikely that a recruit who had been coerced would be sent on an attack of the scale of Mumbai as it might compromise the entire event.

Kasab said that he was previously a laborer and came from a poor family. He said he had been sent on the Mumbai attack by Lashkar and identified two of the plot's masterminds for police.

Kasab told police that the Lashkar group's operations chief, Zaki-ur-Rehman Lakhvi, recruited him for the attack. He also said that the terrorists called another senior Lashkar leader, Yusuf Muzammil, on a satellite phone before the attacks on Mumbai.

The Pakistani Interior Ministry chief told reporters he had no immediate information on Lakhvi or Muzammil.

According to the U.S., Lakhvi has directed Lashkar operations in Chechnya, Bosnia and Southeast Asia, training members to carry out suicide bombings and attack populated areas. In 2004, Lakhvi allegedly sent operatives and funds to attack U.S. forces in Iraq. The US says the Lashkar group has received some of its funding from organizations based in Saudi Arabia and Kuwait, with its leaders making fundraising trips to the Middle East in recent years.

Lashkar was outlawed by Pakistan in 2002.

In further questioning the lone terrorist captured – Kasab told police that 'I have no regrets'. Kasab and the terrorist cell leader began their attacks at the train station – then they later hijacked two cars, before police caught them. He told police he was to seek out 'white targets, preferably British and American'.

Kasab also told police that the terrorists thought they would come out alive and had an escape route.

He said that the ten terrorists, who were highly trained in marine assault and crept into the city by boat, had planned to blow up the Taj Mahal Palace hotel after first executing British and American tourists and then taking hostages. He then added that their intention was to kill 5,000 people. Fortunately for Mumbai - the terrorists armed with plastic explosives - underestimated the strength of the 105-year-old building's solid foundations.

Kasab pretended to be dead, which probably saved his life. It was only when he was being transferred to the hospital by an ambulance that his accompanying security officer noticed he was still breathing. Once inside Nair Hospital, Kasab, who suffered only minor injuries, told medical staff: 'I do not want to die. Please put me on saline.'

Kasab described how he and an accomplice sprayed machine-gun fire around the busy railway station, <u>killing dozens of</u>

people, (official death toll at this location is 10). They planned to attack the exclusive district of Malabar Hill, where they planned to "take VIP hostages" but were killed and injured before they could complete that facet of their mission.

The terrorists were trained over five months in Pakistan occupied Kashmir, and then they had a month off before the attacks. At some point they received intensive instruction in "marine assault" operations.

Kasab and the terrorists, who communicated with each other using Blackberrys during the event, began their journey to Mumbai on November 21.

After Kasab shot up the train station - they hijacked a police 4x4, killing the two officers inside. They continued their killing spree by attacking a gas station and blowing up a taxi before being stopped by security forces.

'I have done right,' he told investigators. 'I have no regrets.'

One police source said: "Kasab was telling our people all of this in a most dispassionate way and responded to the horror on their faces by shrugging his shoulders, as if all of this was of no real consequence."

Kasab will later go to trail in India for his crimes. He will recant this confession. Then during his trial he will recant his - recanting of the confession - admitting to his confession as not being coerced and admitting to the mass murder of innocents as he was trained and directed to target by the Lashkar-e-Taiba Pakistan government involved terrorist group.

Chapter Fifteen

Ordeals of those trapped and hiding

Ordeals of those trapped and hiding:

Briton Richard Farah, who was trapped in his room before being rescued by commandos, hid his passport in his false leg after terrorists were reported to be seeking British and American passport holders to execute.

'I saw all the blood and broken glass and shrapnel. Tons of blood and shoes, people's shoes, women's shoes, men's shoes,' he said. 'In the last few hours there were so many explosions and the floors shook. I said, 'I'm a goner,' because it was right below me. Eventually, we got to the lobby.

Another recount of terrorists hiding with "hostages" - A Briton living in Australia and visiting Mumbai on business - gave a dramatic account of unwittingly being held with two of the terrorists as he and others hid in a darkened room.

He and some 100 guests in the Taj Mahal had taken refuge in a room in the hotel. When the group finally made a dash for the exit - Indian troops shot the two men. One man was thought to be carrying a bag containing explosives. "We did not know they were in the room with us until they tried to escape with us. But the security services knew who they were and shot them." "It was carnage, absolute panic, shouting, screaming and confusion. It was absolutely horrible."

Chapter 16

Final Thoughts

Final Thoughts:

Evidence was emerging last night (December 1, 2008) that the terrorists killed their hostage victims early in the siege and fooled Indian security forces into thinking that they were still holding live hostages. At the Sir J.J. Hospital morgue, a medical official said that of the 87 bodies he had examined almost all had been murdered Wednesday night at the onset of the attacks.

Pakistan's dark Inter-Services Intelligence (ISI) agency was suspected of being behind the 2006 railway bomb attacks in Mumbai and a deadly assault on India's parliament-building four years earlier. This attack brought India and Pakistan to the brink of nuclear war until the U.S. brokered a truce. With the BJP political party demanding hardliner action against Pakistan, the same thing could happen again. This would drag Obama in as a mediator virtually the moment he is sworn in as president. A future BJP political party win in an election might lead to Hindu economic revenge against the Indian Muslim community, pushing more of the population into supporting extremists.

India is 80% Hindu and 18% Muslim.

Another purpose of this event may have been to influence Indian elections as mentioned before but in this scenario the event may have been assisted by the Indian Hindu political "extremist" party called BJP. The reason was to influence the Indian public in the upcoming elections to sway to the anti-Muslim side.

The anti-corruption chief officer (one of the three top officials killed early on in the Mumbai attack – along with the head of the ATS – Anti Terrorism Squad) - was carrying out an investigation into the Samjhota Express "terrorist" attacks. **The**

Samjhota Express incident was masterminded by a serving Hindu-extremist Indian Army Colonel.

Perhaps the BJP Hindu political party assisted in the perpetration of this event in some way - looking to profit by "controlling and channeling the hatred" of the Indian people – after these attacks - towards Kashmir, Pakistan and Muslims.

And also, by murdering the anti-corruption chief - the investigation into the Samjhota Express Event comes to a conclusion with one "mastermind" revealed– the serving Indian army colonel. The investigation does not go any further up a political or military chain of command revealing more government conspirators in a terrorist attack on their own people in their own country with perhaps the international crime boss **Dawood Ibrahim and his D-Gang involvement.**

The purpose of this terrorist attack might have been to provoke an extreme response – nuclear war between India and Pakistan.

Wednesday December 10th, 2008 from USA cable news sources
– headline –
"Pakistan says it is ready to go to war with India"

Due to the "never been seen before" complexity and size of this terrorist event
For the time being India has become an international symbol of organized crime, mass murder and mayhem.

The good men do - dies with them

The evil men do - lives on forever

Epilog

The Turning Point

Will we survive the dark forces planning our destruction - in this new concept and type of war our country is unfamiliar with even recognizing let alone fighting?

There are a couple of different types or kinds of terrorist attacks occurring in the world today. Every attack has its own specific reason for occurring. To look at all of these attacks and group them into one category would be as bad as thinking that all Arabs are Persians or that Ukrainians are the same people as Russians. Arabs are not in your wildest dreams the same people as those that come from Persia. Saudi Arabians are not Iranians. There is a reason they come from different countries, as they are different people

Regarding these attacks, the student of terrorism must ask themselves why, why and why? No one sacrifices their lives for no reason at all.

I'm going to furnish a very short explanation and then a long story to go along with this explanation. Here is a quick synopsis if you would like to skip this section. Fix the situations which create terrorism and terrorists groups and terrorism will go away. Fix the Kashmir property dispute and fix the Pakistan Punjab water issue and this area of the world will heal itself. End of the short story, the long version follows.

1) The first type of terrorist attack is based on some issue, a problem viewed as so severe that blood must be shed. For example: There is a 600 year old property dispute between Pakistan/Islam and India regarding who controls the Kashmir region. Another example is the Israel v Palestine situation. When these unresolved territorial property dispute issues disappear so will the terrorist groups and terrorism.

   a. India and Pakistan have to resolve the Kashmir situation. I feel an independent country of Kashmir would settle this issue of who owns and will govern Kashmir.

- China, Russia and the U.S. must lead this initiative. You are the "big dogs" on the block, show us how large you are and fix this Kashmir situation. Find or make peace in Israel and Palestine and correct the direction in which Africa is headed. Eventually all of these local appearing disputes will have global consequences. We can no longer shrug our shoulders and say: so what….that's happening on the other side of the world and has no affect on my country.

b. The second issue needing resolution between Pakistan and India are water issues caused by dams India has constructed on 2 rivers flowing into Pakistan, suppressing the flow of water into the Punjab region of Pakistan. This may be causing 25K square miles of Pakistan farm land to be starved for water.

c. Israel must assist in the creation of a democratic Palestinian country and these two groups must live in peace.

d. Worldwide, we must find food for people in this part of the world and all parts of the world including Africa. We must be our brother's keeper.

e. Worldwide, people must start practicing some type of birth control and try to have one child per couple. Our world cannot survive if everyone on the planet continues to reproduce at the current rate. And of course, this would violate "the sharia" which also dictates that the man must have as many wives as he can afford and as many children as possible. The world cannot survive at our current rate of human reproduction.

2) The second type of terrorist attack is dictated by "the sharia" code of law. This attack is Muslim on non-Muslim or may be Muslim on Muslim. This document, "the sharia" which surfaced shortly after the death of Mohammad, has two concepts which Western Christians find repulsive.

    a. The first concept Christians find repulsive is that we all must be killed. All non-sharia believing innocents must be mass murdered and a one world Islamic government based on "the sharia" code of law must be created and this is the duty of all Muslims. This document is literally an Islamic license to kill – a Muslim Mien Komft.

- Even though there were no deaths, this type of terrorism is what has occurred in Greece during December of 2008. This type of terrorism is based on causing destabilization of all countries who are not strict followers of "the sharia". Believe it or not, these sharia cult members want all of us dead in America. This strict interpretation also wants all Hindus, Buddhists, and African Tribals eliminated from the face of the earth as their existence is a slap in the face and an affront to their honor as they have no tolerance for anything but who they are.
- Another interpretation of the Greek attacks of December 2008 is that Turkey used the Islamic mosques in Greece as communication centers to orchestrate the multi-faceted fire bombing attacks – which were all perfectly time and target specific coordinated throughout Greece.

Why you ask? Very large oil deposits have been found surrounding Cyprus. Turkey would like nothing better than to see a destabilized Greece that would be unable to assist Cyprus in the coming internal civil war Cyprus will see start sometime in 2010. This civil war will occur when the Pakistan/Afghanistan conflict winds down and frees us jihad assets which can be relocated to cause more mass murder of those who are not "followers".

b. The other concept in "the sharia" that Christians would find repulsive is that females are not allowed to learn or go to school. This effectively turns all females under Islamic rule into slaves with no opportunity for self actualization.

- And again, the penalty for being female and walking to school, as we have just seen in Afghanistan on or about January 15, 2009, is being blinded by acid thrown by the Taliban, who blinded a group of 14 year old school girls on their way to or from school.

The large and first point here is one type of terrorism and terrorist groups can be eliminated immediately by finding a middle ground on the ongoing 600 year property dispute between Pakistan/Islam and India, and to a lesser extent this dispute must include both China and Russia. The property dispute must be also be settled between Israel and Palestine. All property disputes must be settled in Africa, (which is impossible with the oil producing countries of the middle east and Lybia backing this ongoing Islamic terrorist destabilization of the entire continent of Africa).

The second type of terrorism attack can only be stopped by the leaders of the Islamic religion who must show the world their new found religious tolerance with the "rest of the world"

These Islamic religious leaders must rewrite or perhaps just re-interpret a 1.5K year old document and eliminate the concept of "everyone must die who is not a believer in the sharia code of law".

The document may have served this religion well for a period of world history, insuring the survival of their religion. This document, written and interpreted in this fashion, will surely bring the end of this religion when sharia extremists shoot off a nuclear bomb somewhere in the world. The backlash against all of Islam by all countries in the world will be so severe the religion will not survive in its current form.

Mumbai, India has some unresolved issues with Pakistan. There are at least 3 major issues that result in innocent humans dieing in this part of the world.

A) The 1947 partition which created the countries of Pakistan, East Pakistan and India caused the death of 1M unarmed innocent Hindus as they attempted to escape from the "new Pakistan" to the "new India". India has not forgotten this massacre. Perhaps Pakistan and Islam should apologize to India. During this same period of partitioning in 1947, it is estimated that 200K unarmed innocent Muslims are murdered in Jammu, Kashmir by Hindus. Pakistan and Islam has not forgotten this massacre. Perhaps India and the Hindus should apologize to Pakistan.

B) India has recently built dams on 2 rivers which eventually run in the Punjab region of Pakistan. This is starving perhaps 25K square miles of Pakistani Punjab of water for their crops. Perhaps India should release greater amounts of water to their neighbors.

C) There is a property dispute problem in the Kashmir region of India/Pakistan that has an ancient foundation. This property dispute appears to have started in about 1389 to 1413 AD with the rule of Sultan Sikandar Butshikan and his interpretation of "the sharia" code of law, (Right after the end of the Crusades, so to speak)

- The "Tarikh-i-Firishta" historical record of India states that Sikandar passed a law prohibiting anyone but Muslims from living in Kashmir - even though Muslim, Hindu, Sikhs and Buddhist had gotten along together here famously for over 1K years in Kashmir.
- The Tarikh-i-Firishta was written about 1600 AD by Muhammad Kasim Hindu Shah, Firishta - during the reigns of Akbar and Jahangir. It is a generally regarded as one of the best historical records of India. It is based upon earlier Persian historical works.
- The point here is, 1400 AD is the start of problems in the Kashmir area and the property dispute wars appear to have become continuous and have never ceased to this day. These people in this part of the world are still fighting a 600 year war with each other over some property. Currently this area is governed by India, Pakistan and China with Russia sharing a 4th border.
- (This same type of ongoing property disputes between Islam and "the other religions" seems to start during this time also – as there have been an ongoing timeless property dispute in the Southern Philippines between Islam and Christians, an Islamic insurgency in Thailand and an Islam v Tribal war across all of Africa)

I'm going to briefly go over the problems with Kashmir since the 1947 portioning of India by Briton. This story is so large and complicated this tale could and should comprise 2 or 3 books. I typed in Kashmir into Google and this is 1% of the information which came up for me to inspect and relate to you.

- Getting back to the historical problems in Kashmir - during the August 15, 1947 partitioning by Britain which created The Union of India and the Dominion of Pakistan, it was agreed by all parties that Kashmir could chose which country to be included into. It was thought by Pakistan that since the Kashmir region was 75% Islamic that the Kashmir ruler would choose to become part of Pakistan but this was not the case. Pakistan then sent soldiers to destabilize Kashmir to force Kashmir to submit to Pakistan.

- The Maharaja of Kashmir refused Pakistan and signed the Instrument of Accession to India on October 26, 1947, demanding to be governed by India. At this point India sent in soldiers to force out the Pakistan soldiers. Two additional wars are waged between Pakistan and India over the Kashmir area in 1965 and 1969. Pakistan claims that the Instrument of Accession to India on October 26, 1947 was never signed, while India has a copy of this signed document on their web site.

- Kashmir created a Constitution which came into force on January 26, 1957. Elections to the Kashmir Government State Legislative Assembly were held for the first time. This legislature created a Kashmir Constitution which states and demands Kashmir's accession to the Union of India.

- Then in about 1958, Pakistan, in a small western piece of Kashmir under its control, creates its own Kashmir, called "Azad Kashmir". Pakistan also has control of a larger piece of property in the northwest of Kashmir it names the "Northern Areas", (which has no mention in Pakistani laws or its constitution as having any Pakistani status). Then in 1982 the Pakistani President General Zia-ul-Haq officially proclaims to the world that the people of the Northern Areas were Pakistanis. Pakistan claims this property has nothing to do with India, the Indian States of Jammu, Kashmir and Ladakh (the southern and central regions of Kashmir) and the Siachen Glacier.

- In1962, India discovers China has built a road from internal China, Xingjian, through the "Aksai Chin" area of Kashmir, to give China better access to Tibet. China claims this 10% of the Kashmir area as part of China. This causes another war over this area called the Sino-Indian war of October 1962. China apparently has occupied Aksai Chin since the early 1950s and, in addition, an adjoining region comprising approximately 8 % more of the Kashmir territory, accounting for about 10% of the area of the Kashmir.

- In 1963 Pakistan cedes the Aksai Chin territory to China in the Trans-Karakoram Tract agreement. India never recognizes this seizure of 10% of Kashmir by China or Pakistan's authority to cede this area to China.

- A third war is waged in 1972 between India and Pakistan called the Indo-Pakistani War of 1972. India assists East Pakistan into establishing itself as the independent country of Bangladesh. This war leads to the next war as the agreement for peace does not spell out the territorial boundaries for the Siachen Glacier. India and Pakistan sign the Simla Agreement which creates the new country of Bangladesh but it doesn't create a specific boarder between the two countries on the Siachen Glacier.

- Starting on April 13, 1984, is the next Indo-Pakistani property dispute war occurs. This war is over a small part of Kashmir located at 20K feet above sea level comprising about 1K square miles called the Siachen Glacier. This is highest battleground on earth. Both Pakistan and India have forces permanently stationed here at their boarders.

- In 1987, an attack by Pakistan against the Indian army at the glacier is masterminded by Pervez Musharraf who later becomes president of Pakistan. He assaults the Indian troops with an elite commando unit trained by United States Special Operations Forces. They are sent packing after being dislodged from a mountain top at 22K feet by the Indian Army.

- In 1989, an Islamic terrorist insurgency starts in Kashmir which is still ongoing today. It is thought that very large numbers of Islamic Afghanistan Mujahideen fresh from their war with Russia/USSR - the Soviet-Afghan War - and needing a war to fight – moved to Kashmir to fight for Islam against the Hindu/Indian rule of Kashmir.

  - o These people need jobs and food. If they know nothing but killing and war then that is what they are going to continue to do.
  - o The terrorist group called the **Jammu Kashmir Liberation Front** is started by Yasin Malik. This group probably had a hand in the Mumbai Massacre.

- Repeated small wars or battles are fought here, all believed to be initiated by Pakistan in 1990, 1995, 1996 and The Kargil War of 1999. During this time period it is alleged that over 4K rapes of women aged 7 to 70 by Hindu army forces and an additional 4K deaths of unarmed Kashmir citizens occur.

- In 2003, a cease fire on the Siachen Glacier is signed and goes into effect. It is estimated that 4K troops have been killed here by enemy fire and 3K by the elements. It is also estimated that maintaining the military outposts here cost both countries approximately $250M each per year. It is believed there are 150 manned military outposts in this area. The world's highest helicopter pad at Sonam and the world's highest telephone booth are located here on the glacier at 21K feet.

- In 2005 it is estimated that 80K are killed in Kashmir as a result of an earthquake.

- Today, India claims control over about 45% of the Kashmir region. Pakistan claims control of about 35% of the Kashmir region. China claims control of about 10% of this region.

Okay, now what? It is hard for us here in the U.S. to imagine a property dispute like this going on for 600 years. I have an idea. Freeze the boarders where they are for all time and take your military forces home. In the U.S. we have an unguarded boarded with Canada. I guess we in the U.S. should all thank God that we do not have this type of property dispute issues with our northern neighbors in Canada.

But that does not solve the property dispute issues between Pakistan and India over Kashmir. In any event, I see the Mumbai Massacre as being a direct result of this Kashmir property dispute and also a result of the dual massacres of Hindu and Muslim resulting in over 1.2M innocent people being massacred, (which occurred during the partition of India in 1947). There is extremely "bad blood" between the Hindus and Pakistanis. And also, let us not forget the water issue stemming from the dams preventing water flow to Pakistan. And one last issue. If Pakistan and India could feed their population properly there would be no wars – but that is just my opinion.

May I make a suggestion to everyone? "Free" energy will set everyone free. The world is full of free energy for all to use. Create windmills to harness wind power to create free electricity and do the same with solar energy panels. This will create jobs. Set yourselves free as we are about to do in the U.S. Look at what Germany has accomplished in this realm and follow their blueprint for survival. For the $250M per year Pakistan and India each spend on defending the boarder at the 20K foot above sea level Siachen Glacier ..... both countries could build 250 windmills each per year. This free energy I am dreaming of will make all which was once thought impossible – possible.

This is the turning point in the dealing with the dark religious "muzlum" army of mass murderers of innocents, on the loose globally. Islamic religious intolerance has allowed this dark force to bring the mass murder of innocents, death by all means imaginable and destabilization to the world. This is truly the greatest threat to the world currently - the manifestation of Pure Evil.

My hopes are that the new U.S. administration will see the major threat to ours and its own existence – as the transparent – undeclared ongoing worldwide "muzlum vs. everyone else" war – called for by radical interpretations of "the sharia" and bankrolled by the oil producing countries of the Middle East and Lybia.

The stationary fight in Iraq, Afghanistan and Pakistan is to take your attention away from the Pure Evil of the traveling "world terror tour" and the simultaneous ongoing events staged to destabilize across Europe and Africa.

6.5 days after the Mumbai attack ended the 10 to 90 escaped Mumbai terrorists traveled to Greece and staged a Molotov cocktail burning of banks while traveling alongside peaceful college protestors, who are protesting for higher wages. These "Greek/Mumbai terrorists" threw literally thousands of Molotov cocktails in 21 days at banks and businesses across all of Greece and of course - let us never forget the smashing of the Christ figure in the nativity scene. (This is their calling card – it tells us who we are dealing with)

(To the muzlum - western banks are very bad and religiously intolerable - as the Islamic religion and "the sharia" code of law - doesn't allow for a follower of Islam to charge interest)

Imagine the planning – to stage simultaneous events in over 10 to 20 and at one moment 40 towns and cities across 5 countries at once. (Everyone sitting around making a thousand Molotov cocktails preparing for the fire bombing assault on Greece and Europe) Truly unbelievable …but it has just happened in Greece on or around December 11, 2008.

The "muzlum" Islamic World War – I.W.W. is on and happening right now in Greece, India, Pakistan, Afghanistan, Iraq, Saudi Arabia, Somalia, Kashmir and throughout all of Africa and in Mexico – just to name a few locations - and they are wanting to come to your neighborhood to blow you up and kill your children as soon as possible.

Now, with the invasion of the Gaza Strip - the Israeli's have given the I.W.W. a singled positioned focal point. We should all give thanks at night to the state of Israel for momentarily halting Pure Evil in its tracks.

If one has ever studied the development of serial killers or mass murders – you will find they do not start out with mass killings – they evolve into it as they get more comfortable with the aspect of taking innocent life.

The mass murderers of innocents from Pakistan, who murdered in Mumbai, who traveled to attack Greece - will evolve just as a teenage killer of cats may evolve to the murder of humans and then evolve into mass murderers or serial killers.

There are some that believe these dark and evil forces already possess nuclear capability stolen or purchased from the USSR during its decompression in the 1990's.

The next step for this touring army of terror - is to blow something up with a nuclear bomb that went missing from the USSR or given to them as a gift from Iran or North Korea. Or, simply seize the country of Pakistan and launch against India immediately.

Is there really an Islamic World War being waged currently? What are we going to do **when** the muzlumz shoot off a nuke somewhere? The solution to terrorism and finding world peace is as simple as removing the issues which breed this activity.

- Settle the Kashmir property dispute
- Settle the water issues between Pakistan and India
- Find peace between Israel and the Middle East
- Re-interpret "the sharia" to include tolerance of others
- Redirect military funding to create free energy and food
- Fix the situations listed on the following page

A listing of current ongoing Islamic battlegrounds in the
I.W.W.
The Islamic World War

Ongoing Current Islamic conflicts;
- The Oil Wars in Africa including Algeria, Nigeria and everywhere oil is found in Africa
- Insurgency in Saudi Arabia, Bahrain and Egypt including the Sa'dah conflict in Northwest Yemen
- Second Tuareg Rebellion of Mali and Niger
- Darfur, Sudan conflict – incorporating Chad
- The ongoing Ogaden conflict since the 16th century - Ethiopia v Somalia
- Iraq Islamic Civil War
- War in Afghanistan (2001–present) and Pakistan including the ongoing Waziristan War
- The 600 year old Kashmir conflict - Pakistan v India
- Second Chechen War
- Israeli v Palestinian, Lebanon and Gaza Strip conflict including Fatah - Hamas – Hezbollah
- Islamic insurgency in the Philippines from 1400AD
- South Thailand Islamic insurgency campaign
- Kurdistan Workers Party - Kurdish insurgency in Turkey
- War on Terror - U.S.
- The South and Central American Drug Wars and the takeover of Mexico by the Islamic heroin trade